BAD GIRLS

THE INSIDE STORY

BAD GIRLS

THE INSIDE STORY

Jodi Reynolds & Jamie McCallum

HarperCollins*Entertainment*
An Imprint of HarperCollinsPublishers

HarperCollins*Entertainment*
An Imprint of HarperCollins*Publishers*
77–85 Fulham Palace Road,
Hammersmith, London W6 8JB

www.**fire**and**water**.com

A Paperback Original 2001
1 3 5 7 9 8 6 4 2

A catalogue record for this book
is available from the British Library

ISBN 0 00 711548 2

Set in Officina Serif and Sans

Interior design by Design Principals, Warminster, Wiltshire
Printed and bound in Great Britain by
Scotprint, Haddington

Contents

Introduction   6

'All There is' – The Character Profiles   8

The Bile of Bodybag; The Zen of Zandra   40

Series One: The Episode Guides   42

No Giggling: Continuity Shots   62

Series Two: The Episode Guides   64

You Know You're a *Bad Girls* Fan When…   90

Series Three: The Episode Guides   92

Dutch Courage – Shed: The Beginning   106

Where The Buck Stops – The Directors   109

Fertile Territory – The Creation of *Bad Girls*   110

Heavy Steel – The Building of Larkhall   112

Long Johns and Thermal Vests – Secrets from Behind the Scenes   114

A Real Solitary Cell – A Visit to HMP Bullwood Hall   116

The Consultant – Women in Prison   118

The Actors Speak – Cast Interviews   121

'And the Winner is…' – Award Photos   156

Supporting Cast – Ancillary Characters   158

Speaking the Language – Glossary   160

Introduction

Once in a while, a television drama comes along that defies expectations, surprises audiences and confounds critics. *Bad Girls* is one such drama.

First broadcast in May 1999, *Bad Girls* was dismissed by most critics. Parallels were

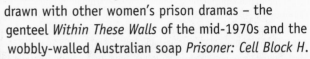

drawn with other women's prison dramas – the genteel *Within These Walls* of the mid-1970s and the wobbly-walled Australian soap *Prisoner: Cell Block H*.

The drama, tragedy and comedy of HMP Larkhall didn't seem to capture the public's imagination either for the first few episodes. Perhaps it just felt a little less cosy and familiar than the reassuring worlds represented by the medical and police dramas dominating the TV schedules. After all, who wanted to settle down for a night's escapism in the secret and often horrific world of a women's prison? Who wanted to witness heroin addiction and decrutching, bullying and suicide, when a dose from a *Peak Practice* doctor made all seem right with the world?

From an initial dip, viewing figures started to rise. And rise. And rise again. After nearly a month of fretting, the *Bad Girls* makers, Ann McManus, Brian Park, Maureen Chadwick and Eileen Gallagher, breathed a collective sigh of relief. Soon, *Bad Girls* was attracting the sort of large audiences that are the stuff of TV chiefs'

dreams. Critics, meanwhile, scratched their heads, unable to comprehend 'the odd popularity of *Bad Girls*'. Audiences had made their own minds up and were hooked – the public's love affair with Larkhall had begun.

As the viewing figures swelled, so did the mailbags. The still somewhat bemused TV chiefs were inundated with thousands of letters and messages. The viewers had spoken, all relating very personal reactions but with a collective theme: not only were they entertained, they were engaged by the way the show challenged their assumptions about prison life and the long-held prejudices about the issues it raised.

Although the stories and characters may often

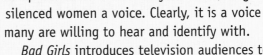

seem larger than life, they are based on extensive research and consultation with the best-informed sources. The aim of *Bad Girls* is to bring women on the periphery of society into living rooms up and down the country: in short, to give silenced women a voice. Clearly, it is a voice many are willing to hear and identify with.

Bad Girls introduces television audiences to an unknown world full of surprising, and often surprisingly likeable, inhabitants. Its predominant and continually developing range of female characters is unique in British drama, from the rough and ready young lesbian, Denny, to Mrs Middle England, Barbara. And, as well as the hardships and horrors of being incarcerated, it portrays the sense of community and companionship that exists in women's prisons. Key to *Bad Girls'* success is the blend of tragic and comic stories, again based on the real-life experiences of women who have been there.

Bad Girls has become one of the country's best-loved dramas, with both viewing figures and a shelfful of awards to testify to this. It has been a success with audiences of all ages, though younger viewers have found it particularly addictive, tuning in to watch in their droves.

Bad Girls may get labelled as a cult success but it's also undeniably a mainstream hit that has millions of viewers. The video sales and internet activity it has spawned (there are over seventy unofficial sites) have been equally astounding. The official website alone – www.badgirls.co.uk – attracted 300,000 hits during the second series. Now even critics have come round, calling *Bad Girls* 'a TV classic of our times' and 'a feminist fable'.

Bad Girls: The Inside Story presents a comprehensive guide to the series. With unique photographs and exclusive interviews with the cast members, creators and company of talents behind the scenes, it boasts unrivalled access to the *Bad Girls* team. Coupled with episode and character guides, insights into the drama's inspiration as well as glimpses of life inside a real prison, *Bad Girls: The Inside Story*, like the show itself, bursts through the bars. 'Welcome to the zoo,' Yvonne tells Barbara in the second series. Indeed. It's visiting time ...

'All there is...'
– The Character Profiles

If there is one element that distinguishes *Bad Girls* from just about any other drama, it is big characters, with big personalities and highly individual voices.

Here the creators of *Bad Girls* give an in-depth insight into the inmates and officers of Larkhall's G-Wing and open some confidential prison files that tell us a bit more about what they really think of each other...

"If she's off the nasty, I'm off chocolate fingers"
Sylvia Hollamby

"Look, all's I did was give her one little kick"
Denny Blood

"Shit happens"
Helen Stewart

"Happiness is door-shaped"
Sylvia Hollamby

"It's a piss off like I told the other tart"
Nikki Wade

"Oh wow, are you both for me?"
Nikki Wade

"Ooh, who slapped her tits"
Zandra Plackett

"At least when Fenner fancies a con, he's got the courage to give her one"
Nikki Wade

"Excuse me while I shit myself"
Shell Dockley

"My dressing gown just slipped off. It's not a crime to have a slippy dressing gown"
Shell Dockley

Nicola Wade

Age: 35   **Sentence:** Life

Personal Background: Middle-class parents: father a senior Naval officer, mother a gin-and-bridge Navy wife. They rejected her when she was expelled from boarding school for 'lesbian activities'. As did her older brother, a married solicitor. Long-term relationship with girlfriend, Trisha, now ended.

Previous Occupation: Club owner

Crime: Killed a policeman who was attempting to rape her girlfriend, Trisha.

Nikki was a lipstick lesbian before the term was invented. She identified her sexuality early in life and has never felt the need to deny or hide it. Her parents' intolerance caused the young Nikki to run away from home, to travel the world in search of a lifestyle.

Nikki was running a successful gay club with her girlfriend, Trisha, when she murdered a policeman by stabbing him in the neck with a bottle. She bitterly regrets the circumstances of her crime but feels badly treated by the legal system, as the rape allegation was not properly investigated.

Most of the inmates in G-Wing look up to Nikki. She is intelligent and street-wise, aware of her external image and the need to protect her status. She has a strong sense of natural justice, because of the injustice she has suffered. Her murder conviction has earned her respect and fear, and she has learned to use this power when dealing with bullying inmates and officers.

Nikki has made a decision not to have her friends visit her in prison – it reminds her too much of what she's missing on the outside and makes it easier to cope with the loss of freedom.

Nikki is no one's fool and, as Helen soon learns, it takes a lot of effort to win her trust. Nikki's fatal flaw, however, is her fierce jealousy which she finds impossible to contain, even to the point of self-destruction.

Officers' Notes:

Name: Nicola Wade

H.M. PRISON LARKHALL

PRIVATE AND CONFIDENTIAL

I remain concerned about Wade's influence on the younger girls e.g. Rachel Hicks. As a new first-time offender, Rachel is easy prey for the likes of this sort of lesbian. I saw her taking Rachel into a corner today and I could see how scared Rachel was. But I have made it clear to Wade I am on to her.

J. Fen...

J. Fenner
Principal O...

Personal Report

H.M. PRISON LARKHALL

Nicola Wade

Contrary to the many reports describing Nikki as a difficult and dangerous loner, I have found her to be intelligent and articulate and concerned for the welfare of her fellow inmates. I see her as a woman of great integrity and passion, for whom confinement is the worst kind of frustration. I am astonished that she has not been recommended for some form of higher education.

Helen Stewart

Helen Stewart
Wing Governor

Personal report

H.M. PRISON LARKHALL

OFFICIAL USE ONLY

If all I ever did in a day was to keep Wade behind bars, that alone would make me proud to be a P.O. Wade is a case in point for the woolly-minded liberals who think 'education is salvation'. All it is for the criminal classes is a way for them to think they're superior to us officers. If it was up to me I would restrict their reading matter to a Gideon and a copy of the prison rules!

S. HOLLAMBY

S. Hollamby
Senior Officer

Michelle Dockley

Age: 27   **Sentence:** Life

Personal Background: Alcoholic mother, Rita, and abusive father. Two daughters, Kayley and Dena, lived with Rita before being taken into care.

Previous Occupation: Kitchen worker

Crime: Shell's in for the kidnap, torture and eventual murder of the woman who 'stole' her boyfriend.

On first appearances, Shell Dockley is the archetypal prison bully. Her ambition is to be queen of the landings and she needs all the little status symbols that life in a prison can offer. Although she would never admit it, she yearns for the respect and the admiration of fellow inmates. She is, however, constantly undermined, and her attempts at bullying are rarely successful. Very often, Shell finds herself alone and isolated, without any real friends.

Her yearnings for attention, status and affection have led her into a self-destructive affair with Prison Officer Jim Fenner. Eventually, through therapy, she acknowledges the cause of her sexual disfunctionality – the years of abuse at the hands of her parents. The act of removing her kids away from her mother and into care demonstrates that she does have an unselfish side. But when therapeutic support is withdrawn, she returns to her old, cold, cunning self.

She has many talents, but perhaps her greatest skill is lying. It makes her a dangerous prisoner because she is always so convincing. She can think on the spot, unlike many of the prison officers who have to deal with her. Shell's not all bad, but some of her jailers would disagree.

<table>
<tr><td>

Officers' Notes:

Name: Michelle Dockley

</td><td>

H.M.PRISON LARKHALL
</td></tr>
</table>

Michelle Dockley continues to give lip, no matter what kindness is shown to her. Clearly the girl's a psychopath. Her wardrobe leaves much to be desired — the two-inch skirts and exposed cleavages. Her homosexual goings-on are enough to turn my stomach. Do management care about GOAD these days? I think not. Also, I think giving a canary to this girl is like waving a chop at a rottweiler.

S. HOLLAMBY

S. Hollamby
Senior Officer

H.M.PRISON LARKHALL

Personal report

Nikki Wade continues to go out of her way to wind Michelle Dockley up. Am glad to see that Michelle is showing maturity in the face of Wade's taunts.

J. Fenner

J. Fenner
Principal Officer

Personal Report

H.M.PRISON LARKHALL

Since Michelle has received her canary she has calmed a ~~great~~ grate deal. She shows a grate deal of maternal instinct to said bird ~~and tells me~~ She talks to him whom she's named Charlie at night and tells me that he is a substitute for her kids while she's inside. Have had to tell her, in no uncertain terms, that I can't pick up special seeds from her friend in Brixton. I think she's beginning to get the message. Just!

Lorna Rose

Lorna Rose
Officer

Daniella Blood

Age: 19   **Sentence:** 7 years

Personal Background: She has a thrice-married alcoholic mother: Jessie Devlin. In care since the age of 5.

Previous Occupation: None

Crime: Arson

Denny has experienced all the corrective institutions. She has been emotionally deprived all her life and was sexually abused by her 'carers'. To compensate, she has formed fiercely loyal, fixated relationships, often with women whom she perceives have power – thus her early obsession with Shell.

Denny's first big crime was to set fire to her children's home; she was being moved out and had fallen in love with the social worker in charge. She didn't want to leave her, so the fire was her protest. After a stay at a young offenders' institution, she was transferred to Larkhall. Despite Denny's violence and outward toughness, she's a rather pathetic character, desperately in need of love and attention. She'll do anything to get the limelight and show off, like the kid she still is.

Denny is a good fighter, being fearless to the point of stupidity. Despite her size, she is strong and works out in her cell and in the gym to maintain her physical advantage. Denny is not very bright and had not learned to read until she came to prison. She is very easily wound up by officers and inmates and can be set up to attack people's enemies.

Officers' Notes:

Name: Daniella Blood

Denny could do better for herself than she does if only she could cut herself off from Shell Dockley. I think lots of our drugs problems on G-Wing are down to Shell using Denny as a runner. I agree with Mr Fenner that Denny doesn't know the truth from lyes and makes things up. Personaly, I think she's been put off men by her father. To the positive, she makes a good Wing Attack at netball, although I've had to give her a bollocking for her bad language on more than one occasion.

Lorna Rose

Lorna Rose
Officer

Personal Report

I like Denny. She's a nice kid with a good sense of humour. She loves her mum and would do anything for her. It's a shame for her that her mum doesn't love her back. She just uses her for her own ends which makes me sick, quite frankly. I'm trying to help Denny see that she has to let go for her own good. Otherwise, she will be taken for a ride and will live to regret it for the rest of her life.

D. Barker

D. Barker
Officer

Yvonne Atkins

Age: 40   **Sentence:** 4 years

Personal Background: Mum to Lauren, aged 20, and Richard (Ritchie), aged 22. Ritchie lives in the South of Spain after a huge fallout with his father. Until she was arrested, Yvonne lived with gangster husband, Charlie, in mock-Tudor splendour in Essex and had a town flat in Chelsea.

Previous Occupation: Betting shop manageress

Crime: Conspiracy to murder: she set up a hit man to knock out one of Charlie's rivals.

Yvonne is as hard as nails: a working-class girl made rich through her husband, Charlie's, criminal gains. Her moral code is simple: don't mess with her or hers – or take the consequences. Yvonne's a mother of two kids: Lauren, on whom she dotes and Ritchie, whom she hasn't seen for two years. She has learned not to talk about him, but she misses him dreadfully.

Yvonne has money and influence. Because things have been easy for her, she has learned to expect to get everything she wants. When people get in her way, she can be ruthless. But there's a generous, warm side to Yvonne. She is free with her possessions and she protects the more vulnerable prisoners from the bullies. The women know they can come to her with their problems and she'll usually find a solution.

She might not be educated, but Yvonne has a razor-sharp brain. She can spot a liar at a hundred yards. She can smell the odour of 'bent screw' hanging in the G-Wing air. No one gets the better of Yvonne in verbal jousts. Her intelligence makes her a danger to the screws. Her status of top dog is one which has the full support of her fellow inmates. Yvonne has a violent streak: it's part of her training as a survivor.

Officers' Notes:

Name: Yvonne Atkins

Since day one, Atkins has been queening it on the landings like she can buy anything she wants. Permitted possessions list?! We might as well tear it up! Carpets, duvets, pelmets – why don't we fit a brass knocker on her cell door? Not to mention a ship-load of musical instruments disrupting good order on the wing! Atkins' whole life has been about lying and cheating her way to the top, which is what she aspires to here. My advice is keep her in her cell/boudoir 24/7 and she won't get her psychopathic tentacles round the other prisoners!

S. HOLLAMBY

S. Hollamby
Senior Officer

Personal Report

They warned us in training about the women winding us up, but they didn't say anything about being bribed with a brand new Harley! (NB –now returned to dealership, refund donated to P.O.'s Retirement Fund.) Yvonne Atkins is very influential on the Wing, not to say powerful. She always gives the impression she could walk out of the front gate if she liked! Which she probably could, given her wealth. On a more positive note, she does look after the vulnerable women and she's been very good with Denny Blood when her mother let her down.

D. McAllister

D. McAllister
Officer

Julie Johnston

Age: 34   **Sentence:** 2 years

Personal Background: Real name: Sonya Dawson. Born to working-class parents, abusive father. Ex-husband, Andy, is in America, with custody of their three kids: Rhiannon (14), Martin (12) and Gary, whom she last saw in nappies.

Previous Occupation: Barmaid, waitress

Crime: Stealing from clients while working as a hotel prostitute with best friend Julie Saunders.

Julie J. felt she was no more than a prostitute in her own marriage, except she didn't even get paid enough to feed her kids. She was forced to take bar work, which is where she met Julie S. Andy wanted his cut of her wages, so she turned, under the protective wing of Julie S., to prostitution. Later they discovered there was ample opportunity to steal from their clients.

Julie J., with Julie S., is constantly in and out of prison; they see it as a rest from their labours. Julie J. justifies her thieving because she fantasises about building a stash of money to go searching for her kids.

Officers' Notes:

Name: Julie Johnston

PRIVATE AND CONFIDENTIAL

Julie J. may not say much for herself but I'm impressed by her inner strength. Even though she does wind me up sometimes with the sexual innuendo, I know she's only doing it for a laugh. I don't think there's an unkind bone in her body – although I suspect the men she robbed would tell a different story! If it wasn't for the support of Julie S., I don't think she'd be able to cope with her husband's abduction of her children. It is possibly only her dream (however unrealistic) of being reunited with her children that saves her from going under.

D. McAllister

D. McAllister
Officer

Julie Saunders

Age: 32 **Sentence:** 2 years

Personal Background: Mother died when Julie was 12. Bullying father is a builder from Billericay. She has a 16-year-old son, David, at boarding school.

Previous Occupation: Hairdressing, waitressing, barmaid

Crime: Caught stealing from clients (with Julie Johnston) while working as a hotel prostitute

Julie S. was forced by her father to separate from her boyfriend, Trevor, when she discovered she was pregnant with David. She was devastated. The Julies met as barmaids when Julie S. had already embarked on a high-earning career as a prostitute.

Julie S. is the boss of their relationship, but she feels protective towards Julie J. and is determined to help her find her kids. She also believes she has psychic powers. She loves to make people – especially Julie J. – laugh, but she can take herself rather seriously.

Julie S. is very proud she has managed to pay for David to go to boarding school but lives in fear of his friends finding out the truth about his mum.

Officers' Notes:

Name: Julie Saunders

OFFICIAL
USE ONLY

If every prisoner was as settled as Julie S., then we could throw away the keys! I wish my own bedroom was as cosy as her's and her pal's! They have such a good laugh together, and bring a great deal of happiness onto the Wing. Sometimes I think that they could get jobs at Butlins as redcoats! If so, I'd be the first in line to rent a chaley!

Lorna Rose

Lorna Rose
Officer

Crystal Gordon

Age: 24   **Sentence:** 12 months

Personal Background: Born in Brixton. Brought up by her single mum. Shared a bedroom with two sisters and a brother – all from different fathers.

Previous Occupation: Shop assistant

Crime: Persistent shop-lifter

Crystal is the moralist on the Wing. As a devout Christian, she takes a critical view of her fellow inmates. She believes the prison regime is too soft and disapproves of the officers' inability to eliminate illicit drugs.

Crystal can be self-righteous and is totally blind to her own self-contradictions. Her initial strategy for survival in Larkhall was to keep her distance from the other inmates. However, although she takes care to hide her emotions, at heart Crystal can be a kind and caring person. She is a virgin, as her mother's sexual activity disgusted her, and she wants to keep herself for the man of her dreams. Josh unleashes the romantic side of Crystal.

Officers' Notes:

Name: Crystal Gordon

Crystal takes self-righteousness to the nth degree, which doesn't help her make friends. She's fiercely anti-drugs, but her zealous attitude and expectation of simple solutions can backfire badly – as with her recent letter to the *Guardian*, which nearly resulted in closed visits. Crystal's heart is in the right place but she tends to feel superior to her fellow inmates. Part of the problem is that she won't take responsibility for her crime and blames the system that put temptation in her way in the first place.

Helen Stewart

H. Stewart
Wing Governor

Zandra Plackett

Age: 20 **Sentence:** 10 months

Personal Background: Zandra's early years were a constant round of foster homes and carers. Her ex-lover, Robin Dunstan, is the father of her baby, Robbie.

Previous Occupation: Drug dealer

Crime: Credit-card fraud

Zandra is one of life's victims. She found happiness for the first time when she met her upper-class boyfriend, Robin. He was in a squat, slumming it for kicks, and they would shoot up together and steal to feed their habit.

Zandra is in prison because she took the rap for Robin, who was in possession of a stash of stolen credit cards. Robin dumped her soon afterwards, returning to the forgiving arms of his parents. Even the arrival of their baby son, Robbie, couldn't melt Robin's heart.

The tragedy in Zandra's life has made it difficult for her to kick her drug habit. However, in prison, she finds the friendship and love she never found on the outside.

Officers' Notes:

Name: Zandra Plackett

Prison has failed Zandra. She came in a junkie and we've done nothing to ensure she won't leave a junkie. She has found friendship here – especially Daniella Blood and Crystal Gordon. Zandra is constantly complaining of ill health. Dr. Nicholson has advised me that all her complaints can be put down to her drug addiction. In my opinion, if we offered Zandra a decent detox programme and proper rehabilitation, she could one day be reunited with her son.

D. McAllister

D. McAllister
Officer

Buki Lester

Age: 17   **Sentence:** 30 months

Personal Background: No known family. Buki has lived in a string of abusive local authority and foster homes. She doesn't have a parent, partner or sibling.

Previous Occupation: Street girl

Crime: GBH – knifed her pimp

Buki Lester is a seventeen-year-old crack head with a history of sexual abuse. She has learned to fight, steal, take drugs and lie compulsively – very convincingly. She had a child when she was thirteen, which was still-born in a public lavatory. She lived rough for a year or two after running away from her last foster home.

Recently, her pimp took her off the streets and put her in a bedsit, but she failed to declare all her tricks and siphoned off money for her drug habit. Her pimp found out about this and beat her up badly. She got her revenge by knifing him. Like many inmates, Buki suffers from very low self-esteem and desperately needs to be valued as a person rather than a commodity.

> **Officers' Notes:**
>
> Name: Buki Lester

A very damaged young woman — history of sexual abuse/drug dependency/zero emotional support/ etc, etc. Good that she is off the streets but am concerned we do not have resources to provide adequate rehabilitation and detox regime. Have located her in a four-bed dorm in hope she will make friends in her age group. Note: she is still self-mutilating. Have assigned P.O. Josh Mitchell as her personal officer to prepare sentence plan.

K. Betts

K. Betts
Wing Governor

Monica Lindsay

Age: 56   **Sentence:** 5 years

Personal Background: A widower with a dependent, thirty-year-old Down's Syndrome son, Spencer.

Previous Occupation: Banking administration

Crime: Convicted of handling £400,000 of stolen funds

Monica arrives in Larkhall a bitter and frantically worried woman. Her real crime was her naivety; her trust and suppressed love for her corrupt employer led her to do things she would never normally consider. Although her crime was not for personal gain, as his financial advisor she was left to carry the can when he fled the country. The only person left in her life is her son, Spencer, whom she has to leave in care.

Someone of Monica's age and class would usually be targeted by the other inmates, but she shows her mettle early and wins their respect. She becomes particularly close to Nikki Wade. Her middle-class background doesn't prevent her empathising with fellow prisoners, and she is soon playing 'mum' to the younger inmates.

Officers' Notes:

Name: Monica Lindsay

PRIVATE AND CONFIDENTIAL

Lindsay is full of airs and graces. She was one of the most difficult receptions we've had in: she refused to submit to a strip-search, on top of her demands to make a phone call home. She hasn't come to terms with the fact that she's a criminal. If there's a lesson to be learned, it's that there's just as many psychopaths with a posh voice as there is not. Despite the fact that she thinks she is a pillar of society, Lindsay is a fraudster through and through.

S. Hollamby

S. Hollamby
Senior Officer

Sharon Wylie

Age: 17 **Sentence:** Life

Personal Background: Lived in Sheffield with her mum, violent step-dad and brother. Best friend is her dog, Molly.

Previous Occupation: Shop assistant

Crime: She murdered three people by spiking the oysters she sold in a supermarket.

Shaz is a happy-go-lucky girl who has no idea of what a life sentence actually means. Extremely immature, she is more interested in the next snooker tournament than dwelling on the fact that her freedom has gone. Shaz has no real handle on her crime. She only intended to get her bullying boss into trouble; to her, it is simply unfortunate that three customers died.

Shaz enjoyed her time on remand, learning tricks from fellow inmates. When she arrives on G-Wing, she actively looks forward to meeting new friends, and immediately strikes up a close friendship and physical relationship with Denny Blood.

Officers' Notes:

Name: Sharon Wylie

PRIVATE AND CONFIDENTIAL

This one needs a ball and chain, if not a padlock on her mouth, if we're to have any hope of rehabilitation. A psychopath to the tips of her unnatural hairdo, she has already cost the tax payer the price of a new hospital vis-à-vis her stupid japes. To think I've devoted the best years of my life doing my civic duty, only to end up running 'married quarters' for the likes of her and Denny Blood?!

S. Hollamby

S. Hollamby
Officer (Basic)

Barbara Hunt

Age: 50   **Sentence:** 3 Years

Personal Background: Married twice. The second time very happily, to millionaire Peter who developed lung cancer. No children from either marriage.

Previous Occupation: Administrator in a Local Authority office

Crime: Manslaughter: the mercy-killing of her husband.

Barbara's life was emotionally empty until she met Peter. In their last months together, she and Peter travelled and enjoyed life until his disease took grip. Under his instructions, Barbara helped him pass away as painlessly as possible. Peter's children from his previous marriage resented their relationship and were angry about the money that was spent in Peter's final months. They accused Barbara of being a murderous gold-digger and their evidence was crucial in her being sent down for manslaughter.

Prison is a huge shock to Barbara; she lived a very active life before, so its restrictions are hard to take. She misses her departed husband very much and is racked by guilt over whether she did the right thing. Helped by cellmate Nikki Wade, she does, however, come into her own.

Officers' Notes:

Name: Barbara Hunt

PRIVATE AND
CONFIDENTIAL

I'm disappointed in Barbara Hunt. At first I had her down as a model prisoner. Hunt's now in with the bricks, so to speak. She's as thick as thieves with the worst prisoner on the Wing: Nikki Wade. Because of Wade's influence, Hunt thinks she can mouth off as much as she likes. She's certainly got enough to say in that diary of hers. I'm keeping my eye on her.

J. Fenner

J. Fenner
Principal Officer

Helen Stewart

Age: 30   **Grade:** Governor Grade 4

In Service: 5 years   **Previous Occupation:** Temped as a student

Personal Background: Helen was brought up by her widowed father, an austere Presbyterian minister, who never showed her much love. She has had many boyfriends, the latest being landscape gardener Sean Parr, but she is ambivalent about full-scale commitment and marriage.

Because of her family background, Helen has wanted something structured in her life, to feel she can make an impact. She has a deep-rooted sense of natural justice and an instinctive empathy for those women on the inside who have been dealt a rough hand in life.

Helen's personality is complex and contradictory. She is talented and supremely able but suffers from external prejudices and internal demons. She wants to run a fair regime which can be seen to be fair by all who live and work under it. She can, therefore, sometimes be a bit of a stickler for the rules. Her uncompromising stance doesn't go down well with many of the inmates, or with some of her colleagues – especially Jim Fenner, whose activities on the Wing require a much more lax regime than anything Helen will allow.

Helen's strong belief in justice prevents her from being a rule-twister. She is warm and generous and can often be reduced to (private) tears when she comes up against the prejudices of the prison's old-boy network. She also has great empathy for her charges: their life stories and problems take their emotional toll on Helen. She is an excellent judge of character and relies on her instincts even when the facts tend to suggest she may be wrong – which is why she is so drawn to Nikki Wade.

Staff Appraisal Notes:

H.M. PRISON LARKHALL

Name: Helen Stewart

Plus Points:

A bright girl; dedicated to her career; determined to be 'innovative'; a visible presence on the Wing — full complement of staff or no!; not afraid to be unpopular with staff and inmates alike; speaks her mind, uninhibited by her youth and inexperience.

Minus Points:

Apt to hysterical overreaction; cold and aloof with colleagues; poor judge of character; unwilling to benefit from others' experience; chip on shoulder; uses her position to promote 'politically correct feminist' politics; averse to constructive criticism; disregard for the conventions of formal dress.

S. Stubberfield
Governing Governor

Memorandum

H.M. PRISON LARKHALL

FROM: Jim Fenner
TO: Simon Stubberfield

Dear Simon,

Congratulations again on your birdie at the ninth. That is a pint I owe you! On a Larkhall matter — just thought you should know that G-Wing's attendance at your fashion show has been cancelled. I think Miss Stewart may be unaware of the kicking-off this will cause, as well as your VIP guests asking what's going on. As I said to you in the clubhouse, we've really got to be on our guard that G-Wing doesn't become cast adrift from the rest of Larkhall and get turned into some sort of experiment for fast-track theory. I'm on my pager if you need me.

Yours,
Jim

Jim Fenner

Age: 42   **Grade:** Principal Officer

In Service: 20 years   **Previous Occupation:** Army

Personal Background: Separated from wife, Marilyn, after 8 years of marriage. Two children: Tom (7) and Becky (6). His mother and father live a few miles away from Jim's home and still think he is happily married.

Jim is the P.O.'s P.O. He has eased into a way of working which gives him a comfortable life. The women in his charge have that little bit of extra leeway. He doesn't take things too seriously and encourages his colleagues not to get too uptight about things – they've all got lives outside to get on with.

The smarter inmates on the Wing see right through Jim, but to the ordinary prisoner, like the Two Julies, Mr Fenner is all right. He's easy-going and has a studied air of caring. They believe he doesn't talk down to them, and take his fake concern at face value.

Jim's a popular man with the prison officers too. They consider him wise, but not too much of a clever-dick. There's a self-deprecating front to him. He likes to say he doesn't have all the answers, although he actually believes he does.

Helen's firm-but-fair regime is too restrictive for Jim. There are too many reports, adjudications and punishments which Jim feels are petty, do nothing to promote good order and cause all kinds of hassle for him and his colleagues. Jim pretends to cooperate with Helen's regime, with a grudging acceptance. In fact, as often as he can, he subtly undermines her to his fellow officers and to prisoners alike.

Until Shell spiked his cover, Jim considered himself a very happily married man, on his own terms. He's devoted to his two children, and his wife, Marilyn, had no cause to complain. The fact that Jim's had several sexual relationships with prisoners in his care doesn't bother him too much. He can easily justify his 'pastoral' role; the women have come on strong to him, he's got what they need and he's happy to give it to them. So where's the harm?

Officer Appraisal Notes:
Name: Jim Fenner

H.M. PRISON LARKHALL

Plus Points:

Exceptionally safe pair of hands; immensely popular with staff and the girls; never talks over the girls' heads; first-rate in a crisis; calm influence at all times – even in face of extreme provocation from inmates or colleagues!; clubbable chap – plays mean round of golf.

Minus Points:

Underestimates his own potential (fear of failure?); suspicious of new ideas; could be more proactive on professional development front (suspect domestic constraints on attendance re. residential courses!)

S. Stubberfield
Governing Governor

H.M. PRISON LARKHALL

Memorandum

PRIVATE AND CONFIDENTIAL

FROM: LSLG Helen Stewart
TO: GG Simon Stubberfield

Prior to our meeting tomorrow, I want to put on record my anger that Jim Fenner has returned to his duties on G-Wing. It is my firm belief – despite the fact that there are to be no criminal charges – that he assaulted Michelle Dockley in her cell. I suggest we transfer Mr Fenner to another Wing although I would prefer him to be given non-residential duties. G-Wing now needs a period of calm and stability. Mr Fenner's presence here will aggravate an already tense situation.

HS

Sylvia Hollamby

Age: 53 **Grade:** Senior Officer

In Service: 12 years – with several career breaks for parenting and sickness

Previous Occupation: Traffic Warden

Personal Background: Husband, Bobby, an ex-prison officer, runs a funeral parlour where Sylvia sometimes helps out. They have three children: Constance (30), who is married with one child, called Constance; Gayle (28); Bobby Darren (21). They live in Streatham.

Sylvia is the cynic in the prison office, the epitome of the 'never listened, never learned' officer. She has no respect for expert opinion whatsoever and despises the fact that Helen seems to want to be the 'prisoners' friend'.

Sylvia always thinks the worst of people and their motives and, no matter what, always feels hard done by. Although she constantly moans about her job, the truth, however, is that she loves it. It's an easy life for her: sitting around in the office, being served tea by the prisoners and bad-mouthing other folk.

Prison would be just fine for Sylvia if it weren't for the prisoners – and, of course, a few of her officer colleagues as well. She has no sympathy for any of the inmates, regarding them all as guilty psychopaths who will never change their ways. She cares not a jot that they're banged up. If it were up to her, that's where most of them would stay. To Sylvia, happiness is door-shaped.

Very occasionally, Sylvia shows some redeeming characteristics: a genuine loyalty to Jim Fenner and shedding a tear at the birth of Zandra's baby. But, generally, Sylvia does an excellent job at keeping any kindness in check and the spirit of Thatcherism alive.

Officer Appraisal Notes:

Name: Sylvia Hollamby

Try as I might, I find it almost impossible to write something positive about Senior Officer Hollamby. There is more than a hint of the jackboot in her approach to the women. Her attendance record is poor. She's indolent and obstructive. She has a bunker mentality and greets any innovation as a threat, as if the prison should be run for her own comfort and convenience. Perhaps her only saving grace is that she prides herself on a moral code that would make her incorruptible for her own personal gain. However, a modern prison service needs more – much more – from its officers.

Helen Stewart
Wing Governor

Senior Officer Hollamby is one of the main reasons G-Wing is run so smoothly: commitment and professionalism in equal measure. Thanks must be paid to her for her loyalty to her colleagues. She recognises that common sense, not academic degrees, are what you need for this job. She also knows the most important weapon that management has is the staff, whose dedication stops a downward spiral of problems amongst the prisoners. Senior Officer Hollamby doesn't try to be popular with either management or the girls, but what's the problem with that, I ask? Everybody knows where they stand with her. Surely, in these days of back-scratching and brown-nosing, that's a good model?

J. Fenner
Principal Officer

BAD GIRLS

Karen Betts

Age: 38 **Grade:** Wing Governor (Grade 5)

In Service: 6 years **Previous Occupation:** Nurse

Personal Background: Joined the WRAF aged 17 and qualified there as a state-registered nurse. She joined a London hospital but left for the prison service. She is a divorcee with a grown up son, Ross, who is at university.

Karen is a self-made, working-class woman. She met her husband, Dennis Betts, in the WRAF and married him after she became pregnant with Ross. Their marriage didn't last. Her last partner, Steve, a P.O., introduced her to the prison service, and she changed careers from nursing, to gain security and income to support her son.

Karen seized every opportunity the prison service offered and discovered a latent ambition in herself. She successfully completed a part-time B.A. in sociology, and believes that education is the key to freedom. Karen's great advantage as a Wing Governor is that she has come up through the ranks. She has no patience with the old-style union culture of the Prison Officers' Association but, unlike Helen, she tempers her reformist zeal with pragmatism. Her flaw is that, despite all the warnings, she still finds herself falling in love with smooth-talking bastards.

Staff Appraisal Notes:

Name: Karen Betts

In the few months she has been in the post, Miss Betts has successfully stamped her fragrant authority on G-Wing. She is in charge of some of the most difficult prisoners in Larkhall, but has left no doubt as to who is running the show. Miss Betts and I are very relieved that the allegations against Mr Fenner have proved unfounded. I'm certain they will make a formidable team — just what this troubled Wing requires.

S. Stubberfield
Governing Governor

Dominic McAllister

Age: 23   **Grade:** Officer (Basic)

In Service: Nearly 1 year   **Previous Occupation:** Student (dropped out)

Personal Background: Single; lives with his mum, Frances, and dad, Stephen, in a small terraced house in Merton. He is on the lookout for a girlfriend and is saving up to get a place of his own.

Dominic is not the brightest of sparks, but he's kind towards the women, and they respect him for that. But they also sense his awkwardness – especially where matters of a sexual nature are concerned – and enjoy having a little fun at his expense.

The inmates know that Dominic doesn't like punishing them with bang-ups and loss of remission. Perhaps this means he is a soft touch, but he's also incorruptible. Only someone with Dominic's credentials would sense something wrong with Jim Fenner. His positive attitude and dedication to the women make him an excellent officer.

Dominic is not afraid to speak his mind about the petty barbarities of prison life. Sylvia's views make him squirm and he's often in conflict with her. It's true that Dominic fancies Helen, but he seems unable to encourage any interest.

Officer Appraisal Notes:

Name: Dominic McAllister

As to the positive, Dominic is making progress since his early days here, but he still has much to learn about the criminal mind. He must learn that this job is not about fancy theories and trendy therapies, it's about locking doors!

Dominic has got to watch out that he is not seen by the prisoners as an easy touch. He is a bit too gormless for his own good and they'll take advantage. At this juncture, in my opinion, Dominic could either sink or swim, dependant on him changing his attitude.

S. Hollamby
Senior Officer

Lorna Rose

Age: 25 **Grade:** Officer (Basic)

In Service: 1 year 10 months **Previous Occupation:** Bakery assistant

Personal Background: Lorna lives with her mum and dad on a modern estate in Wandsworth. Her brother, Kenneth, lives with his wife and child down the road. Lorna has never had a partner and is scared to go to gay bars in case she'll meet ex-inmates.

Lorna's job gives her enormous satisfaction. She loves the uniform and telling 'the girls' what to do. There's a status and security that comes with being a prison officer – and Lorna remembers only too well those dark days selling doughnuts at the bakery; she doesn't want to go back there.

Lorna is pretty thick and the women know it. She has a natural, masculine swagger and likes to throw her weight about, threatening physical reprisals if the women step out of line; it's all part of her 'Cock-of-the-Walk' demeanour.

In her bid to be everyone's favourite screw, Lorna has to make concessions. Once she has stepped over the line, she is taken advantage of. Ultimately, she pays a very high price.

Officer Appraisal Notes:

Name: Lorna Rose

Lorna has got jail craft in her blood. I see in Lorna my young self – enthusiastic, loyal, good communicator – so long as the present regime doesn't knock it out of her! Lorna is as streetwise as the cons, which is a great strength. Her ambition is to join the DST, but I think she would be a loss to the landings and have advised her accordingly. I recommend this officer for early promotion to Senior Officer asap a vacancy exists.

J. Fenner
Principal Officer

Simon Stubberfield

Age: 55   **Grade:** Governing Governor

In Service: 20 years   **Previous Occupation:** Civil Servant

Personal Background: Simon lives in Fulham with his wife, Stella. They have two children, Simon (29) and Emma (25).

Simon strives to look the part of governor, so loves media appearances and impressing those with influence. He is both ambitious and indolent. His sights are set on promotion to Area Management and he'll do anything to keep his reputation unsullied. This is why he cannot be relied on to run a fair regime.

Rather than visiting the wings, Simon is the kind of governor who prefers to run things from his office. When things go wrong, he'll look for scapegoats, but he'll always take the credit when things go well.

Simon relishes his status in the community. He is a dutiful husband and father, president of his golf club, Master Freemason and active supporter of his local church.

Staff Appraisal Notes:

Name: Simon Stubberfield

Mr Stubberfield has shown himself to be a man with his hand on the tiller. One only needs to walk the corridors of Larkhall to see what a well run regime is in place. The prisoners seem happy, the officers relaxed, and it's clear that Mr Stubberfield goes out of his way to promote harmony within the prison. His promotion of the excellent work being done in the prison service is first class. My wife and I thoroughly enjoyed the recent fashion show!

M. Caulder
Area Management

Di Barker

Age: 32   **Grade:** Officer

In Service: 8 years   **Previous Occupation:** Job Centre clerk

Personal Background: Di is single and lives with her invalid widowed mother, Dorothy, in a terraced house in Tooting.

On the surface, Di is a jolly person who enjoys the camaraderie of her colleagues and genuinely feels for the inmates. Di likes to think her sunny nature bathes G-Wing in a warm, friendly glow. She wants everyone in the prison to be part of a happy family – with her wrapped in its bosom.

The truth is that Di is seriously screwed up. After years of dutiful self-sacrifice, looking after her mother, Di is desperate to find a man who will help her escape to a new and fulfilled life. She blames her mother for spoiling her chances, and her mother suffers for it.

The tedious drudgery of Di's life infects her whole outlook. The bright smile is a front for a deep-rooted hysteria, which leaks out from time to time when things go wrong on the Wing. Di has no social, sex or love life. Her home is her personal prison; Larkhall is her only place of freedom. The demands made upon her by her dependent mother eat away at her, until she's verging on a serious nervous breakdown. All this she keeps hidden from the world.

It's not just that Di pretends to others that things are all sweetness and light; she pretends to herself as well. She doesn't know that she's actually full of self-loathing. She sees her obsessions with individual men as adult, reciprocated relationships. She sees potential rivals for her men's affections as two-headed monsters. Her desperate need for love makes her a ruthless enemy if anyone gets in her way.

Despite her mental-health problems, Di is a survivor. Her mind becomes calculating when she's cornered and she can speak up for herself if she doesn't get her own way. Di works hard at her job, she loves it and she's good at it. If she could only be free of her burdens, she might grow into a normal human being.

Officer Appraisal Notes:

Name: Di Barker

H.M. PRISON
LARKHALL

How could I speak ill of an experienced landings officer and good
P.O.A. member like Di Barker? The sad gap after we lost young Lorna
Rose could not have been filled better than by her. If I have a small
criticism I would only say Di veers a bit too much on the soft side
with the inmates as in she is too 'touchy-feely' by half!! For her own
good I've advised her to just watch that she doesn't leave herself
wide open, especially with being Personal Officer to the likes of
cunning perverts like Wade.

S. Hollamby
Senior Officer

Officer Appraisal Notes:

Name: Di Barker

H.M. PRISON
LARKHALL

Let me say at the outset that Officer Barker is a good P.O. – she
turns up on time and she works 12-hour shifts and still stays smiling
(even if it's bedwatch!). If you need your shift covering at short
notice, Officer Barker will be the first to offer. If Di does have a
problem, it's maybe that she volunteers to do too much (you've got to
have a meal break, Di!). She sometimes overstretches herself and the
girls quickly pick up the fact that she is near to losing it. Maybe
it's hormone-related, but there is a school of thought that Officer
Barker brings it on herself. Having said that, the girls relate well
to her. She gives them a lot of her time and, although she gets the
mickey taken, you can see they know that she's got a good heart.

J. Fenner
Principal Officer

Gina Rossi

Age: 26 **Grade:** Officer

In Service: 2 years **Previous Occupation:** Barmaid

Personal Background: Gina lives with her on-off boyfriend, Mark, in the prison officers' flats close to Larkhall. Her mother is dead but she has a doting father, Enzo, and two younger brothers, Romani and Marcello, who live with their dad in Stockwell.

Gina is a good-looking woman of Italian stock, born and bred in London. She's in a tempestuous relationship with her boyfriend, Mark, who works on D-Wing. Mark is the love of her life and, although she's a huge flirt herself, she gets madly jealous if he so much as looks at another woman. Gina knows Mark thinks the world of her and this makes her highly aware of her sexual allure.

Quick-witted and fun, Gina is the one who'll organise the social functions and make a fool of herself at them. She's a good P.O.A. member, but isn't a dinosaur like Sylvia. Gina's main problem is her temperament. No matter how much she tries to control herself, she never succeeds, and may live to regret it.

Officer Appraisal Notes:

Name: Gina Rossi

Despite my initial misgivings, Gina shows a good attitude to the job. She gets on well with the inmates but knows where to draw the line. A lively personality and a good organiser, she lifts the spirits on the Wing. Have warned her to watch the temper and keep her love life to off-duty; so far no flare-ups and has kept her fists to herself. Attendance v. good, time-keeping not so, esp. on earlies. Overall, looks like the move from D-Wing has been a success.

K. Betts
Wing Governor

Josh Mitchell

Age: 24 **Grade:** NEPO (New Entrant P. O.)

In Service: Starter **Previous Occupation:** Window cleaner; prison works department

Personal Background: Josh lives in Acton in a mate's house; his mate is abroad and Josh pays his mortgage for a share of the profit when it's sold. Josh is the apple of his mum, Petra's, eye. His dad left when he was three. His younger sister, Janet, lives in Stoke Newington.

Josh is an easy-going, but not lazy, guy. He cares about the prisoners in his care, possibly because he can easily see himself in their position. He knows the difference between right and wrong, but he's got his own set of beliefs which informs the way he thinks about life and his job. Okay, so he's brought in a few dodgy items for the prisoners. So what? No one's going to get hurt and that's the important thing for him.

Josh is hugely popular with the women, but he uses his humour to hide the fact that he's out of his depth with them. Although he's very attractive and attracted to women, he's a one-woman man and Crystal is the one.

Officer Appraisal Notes:

Name: Josh Mitchell

Josh is making a great start in his first weeks on the landings. Personally, I never doubted he would be made for the uniform. He is making a very good impression on staff and inmates alike, not to mention a great pot of tea!! If I have any criticism at all, it is only that he must be careful he isn't too smiley with the girls as this could lead to being manipulated. But I have no doubt that he will learn to be as good at the discipline as he is on the likeability front and will make all my training effort well worthwhile.

D. Barker
Officer

The Bile of Bodybag

'My Bobby's doing his braised meatballs tonight. I've been salivering all day'
Serving suggestion from the Hollamby kitchen

'You watch. She'll be out of that uniform into a suit faster than Clark Kent'
A patented Bodybag demonstration in how not to be bitter

'She's got more chance of coming off the nasty than I have of being invited up to Cliff Richard's hotel room for cream cakes and sex!'
The secret fantasy life of Sylvia Hollamby, allied with her strongly held belief in rehabilitation

'Then it's back to the girlfriend for him and the same for her!'
Visiting day neatly summarised by an insightful Sylvia

'You don't have to be George Clooney to work out the diagnosis here'
Sylvia exhibiting her lamentable lack of medical diagnostics with regard to Zandra's symptoms

'Zandra Plackett's got more junk in her than Steptoe's back yard'
Sylvia muses when 'spring cleaning' Zandra's cell

'When God was handing out the singing voices to your people, you must 've been somewhere else'
Hollamby reveals her more enlightened side

'As if it's the highlight of my day to peer up women's smelly bottoms'
Sylvia tells it like it is

'What are you after? A gold star?'
The Bodybag appraisal of people who agree with good ideas

'Could we have a murder every day please?!?!'
Sylvia's contribution to the Larkhall suggestion box on how to run a prison effectively

'Happiness is door-shaped as far as I'm concerned'
Hollamby proving she's a woman who knows what she likes...

'Well, that's as clear as a cloud'
Sylvia is unimpressed by Helen's management speak

The Zen of Zan (RIP)

'What would be interesting is if it didn't take half a day to go through this BORING BOLLOCKS!'
Zandra expresses her dissatisfaction with the prison reception process

'Pull the other one, it farts Elvis!'
Zandra gently questions the validity of the two Julies' logic

'Give up? In here? Yeah and the Pope buys French ticklers from Tesco's'
Zandra articulates the difficulties of giving up drugs in a prison environment.

'Wondering how I did it inside? Why do you think they call them screws?'
Ms Plackett's calm riposte as to how she managed to get up the stick on the inside, much to the chagrin of Dominic

'Lord Longford maybe, him up there don't give a shit!'
Zan points out to Crystal that her faith in THE Lord might be misplaced

'Ooooh! Who slapped her tits?'
Zandra patiently endeavours to find the reason behind Denny's seeming distress

'Like a stick of Blackpool twatting rock, what do you think I mean?'
Lorna's fears that Zandra asked her to bring back drugs and not confectionery from holiday are swiftly dispensed with

'Come on you twatting twat! I said come on!'
The Plackett approach to the opening of an obdurate window

'If Shell told her to live in a barrel of shit she'd do it'
Zandra proposes that sometimes, just sometimes, Denny is apt to be a little influenced by Shell Dockley

'He says I'm putting it on. I mean, what would he do if he woke up to find a dead girl swinging from the window with her tongue licking her knees?'
Zan employs reason to illuminate why it might be appropriate for her to receive some form of prescribed medication for her nervous disposition

'Yeah well, there'll be a bed for her in here in fifteen years' time won't there?'
Zan expresses her enduring faith in human nature

EPISODE 1 SERIES 1

Amid the preparations for a prisoners' fashion show, idealistic new Wing Governor Helen Stewart is catapulted into her first major crisis. A young prisoner is left unattended, despite her cries for help, and suffers a miscarriage. Feelings are running high on the Wing as word gets out, but Helen is unable to prove the staff negligence she correctly suspects.

Against the advice of her senior officer, Jim Fenner, Helen decides to face the women and call a meeting on G-Wing. She reassures them of her deep regret at the tragedy but tells them that no officer was to blame: it was a 'tragic set of circumstances'. The anger of the inmates boils over and a near riot ensues. Lifer Nikki Wade steps out of the fray and articulates the women's protest – the staff in Larkhall prison are incompetent and the system is a disgrace. Why should the prisoners make the staff look good by parading in costume in front of the great and the good?

Helen is forced into a corner and calls Nikki's bluff. She cancels the Wing's participation

in the fashion show. The women are in uproar. They have worked hard on their costumes and the event has provided a welcome diversion in the otherwise stifling regime. In an instant Nikki has lost the support of her peers and her minimal freedom, as Helen orders her on to the segregation block – Nikki's on 'Rule 43'. Gleeful officers roughly escort her away.

Fenner again reasons to Helen that by punishing the women she will only incite more bitterness and resentment. It will also go down very badly with the Governing Governor, Simon Stubberfield. Jim's concern however is not entirely selfless. Shell Dockley, his bit on the side, is willing to persuade Jim, the best way she knows, that the fashion show must go on.

Jim exploits the 'old boy network' and alerts Simon Stubberfield to Helen's hot-headed decision on the Wing. Simon summons Helen and gives her only one option – back down and reinstate the fashion show. In turmoil, Helen returns home to her fiancé Sean, who is supportive but unable to fully comprehend her predicament. She should swallow her pride and do what Simon says. Helen is very much alone.

In Larkhall, meanwhile, solitude is harder to come by. Rachel Hicks, a vulnerable new inmate endures the incessant bullying of her cellmate, Denny Blood, sidekick to the equally violent 'top-dog', Shell. With 'victim' written all over her, it seems the teenager's only salvation may come from Jim Fenner. Jim's protection comes at a price. It's a price Rachel,

terrified and desperate for comfort, is seemingly willing to pay.

By morning, Helen's decision is made. She will use the archaic system to her own advantage, by appealing to the one person who is even more contemptuous of it than she is – Nikki Wade.

Helen's plan initially falls on deaf ears. Nikki has seen and experienced too much of prison life to be anything but sceptical. But Helen perseveres and tries to convince her that she intends to make changes to the way things are done at Larkhall, but to succeed she'll need co-operation. Nikki's anxious that the prisoners do not lose out and finally agrees to help.

Helen gets Nikki out of the segregation block and Nikki announces to the Wing that a deal has been struck. The fashion show will take place on the promise of the women's good behaviour. Nikki has given Helen her personal assurances. The conflict is diffused and replaced immediately by the excitement of the upcoming event. Helen is grateful, but Nikki makes it very clear that her collaboration was aimed at helping her fellow prisoners, not the Wing Governor.

It's jubilation all round, except when Shell sees her 'designer' dress walking out on the back of recidivist shoplifter, 'Smelly' Nelly Snape. The two guilty Julies have some sewing to do...

And so the show goes on and the normally drab prison is for once enlivened with colour, spectacle and hope. Shell, dressed to kill in her new costume, works her audience and revels in the limelight and the good order of the Wing, for now at least, is restored. The VIP audience, to Simon's relief, is suitably impressed and Helen has secured a small victory, if not won the war. As the festivities end and as the cacophony of nightcalls begins, Rachel has finally escaped the terror of sharing a cell with Denny. In her place she has a new companion for lights out: Jim Fenner.

EPISODE 2 SERIES 1

Helen is determined that the high level of drug abuse in G-Wing must be tackled. An anonymous tip off has alerted her that their random drug testing is anything but random. She's shocked to learn that known users are avoided to make the figures look better. Fenner scoffs at her naivety – all prisons massage their statistics. A lot less paperwork and a lot less trouble from the Home Office. Besides, he jeers: 'Prison makes them feel bad and drugs make them feel good'. The Wing Governor however is resolute. She institutes a campaign encouraging inmates to report pushers to the feared, military-styled Dedicated Search Team (DST).

Helen's campaign gives Shell Dockley an idea. Shell bullies Rachel to write a letter falsely naming Nikki Wade, Shell's arch-enemy, as a pusher. Shell, very pleased with herself, has ensured the DST will have their first hit. Into the bargain, the cowering Rachel won't

quickly forget just who is boss on the landing.

As Helen's drug initiative gets off to a shaky start, yet another young addict, Zandra Plackett, disembarks from the cattle truck. Shivering from the rain and desperate for a fix, she becomes increasingly agitated by the drawn-out admissions process. Sharing her distress is Monica Lindsey, another new arrival. Middle-aged and middle-class, she is bewildered and incensed at the dehumanising procedures facing new inmates. Monica is desperate to make a phone call, Zandra is desperate for gear, the staff are desperate to get home for the weekend.

Zandra and Monica spend a miserable weekend holed in the unsanitary and dismal reception dorm. Finally, staff allocate Monica and Zandra to their new homes – both are to go on G-Wing. Monica is desperate just to get there to make her call. Zandra is distraught – she has enemies in G-Wing with old scores to settle. Her pleas to be put into another wing fall on deaf ears.

Zandra's worst fears are realised when she and Monica are put into the four-bed dorm with Denny Blood – the very inmate she needed to avoid. Denny reckons Zandra swindled her out of a drugs stash during her last visit to Larkhall. As Denny prepares to throttle the beleaguered Zandra, Monica snaps out of her comatose state and slaps Denny's face. Denny's too stunned to respond. How could a posh old woman dare to hit a top Larkhall bully?

By the time Monica is escorted to Helen's office for her formal induction, she is inflamed and launches into a tirade against the regime. Helen is bemused by Monica's attitude: she simply wants to help ease Monica's transition into prison life. Monica explains that she has

a Down's Syndrome son, Spencer, who completely relies upon her. For two days she has been unable to phone him to explain where she is. Helen recoils and apologises. Monica doesn't want her pity or the anti-depressants she has suggested. Why should her burden be eased when Spencer's can't?

Shell's plan for Nikki succeeds as Nikki is stripped and searched for drugs by the sadistic DST. Meanwhile Shell and Denny are carrying out their own intimate search for drugs on the defenceless Zandra in the shower room of G-Wing. When Monica returns to the dorm she discovers a hunched and sobbing Zandra. Nikki, still smarting from her own maltreatment, is left to explain that Zandra has been de-crutched for her drugs.

Fenner enjoys telling Helen that her favourite inmate has been the first victim of her new tough regime on drugs. Helen is horrified and visits Nikki in her cell to apologise. As Nikki tries to salvage the vestiges of her pride, she is unreceptive to Helen. Her moral high ground in tatters, Helen is no nearer to establishing Nikki as an influential ally amongst the inmates.

The new inmates keenly anticipate visiting time. Zandra is expecting a drugs parcel and Monica, her son. Monica tries to console Spencer by explaining that she is doing a very special job for the queen. His disappointment is as palpable as her guilt. Zandra has more immediate concerns. Her fiancé, and therefore her fix, do not show. The officers are unsympathetic. She causes a scene.

A bigger scene swiftly erupts, however. The DST, who are supervising proceedings, detect a drugs exchange and swoop violently on the perpetrators. The visiting room is plunged into mayhem and a terrified Spencer is left screaming. The two Julies come to the rescue by getting everyone in the visiting room to clap, to pretend to Spencer it's all a child's game. Monica can't believe the pain and suffering she has visited on her innocent son.

The pandemonium spills back into the Wing and the prisoners' association time is cancelled. All Helen can do is apologise to her staff for the disruption caused by the clumsiness of the DST. She concedes that her strategies must be reviewed. Fenner meanwhile is delighted at her failure.

EPISODE 3 SERIES 1

With Helen's drug strategy in disarray, Zandra is free to pursue her drug addiction with little obstruction. Monica warns it will kill her, but to Zandra it's a risk that is offset by her need for escapism.

Meanwhile, Rachel is relying on her own chosen method of survival: Jim Fenner. Jim has bestowed attention on her and, she mistakenly believes, protection. Fragile Rachel has convinced herself she's in love with him. This devotion is extremely convenient for Jim but his predatory actions do not go unnoticed. Nikki tries but fails to warn Rachel off him. But much worse for Rachel, Shell Dockley, Jim's long-standing bit on the side, begins to suspect the liaison.

By visiting day, Zandra is counting on her fiancé, Robin, to smuggle in her next fix. Robin is empty-handed and informs her that he has committed to a detox programme. He has moved on – which is the very thing that Zandra, stuck in the Larkhall dolls' house, cannot do. Feeling betrayed, Zandra realises that sharing an addiction was the basis of their relationship. While her cellmates dismiss her sobbing as simply 'boyfriend trouble', Zandra faces more serious life choices.

Zandra resolves to make Robin proud; she will concentrate on beating her addiction. She has failed to realise that she must conquer her addiction for no one else but herself, and intends her actions to be a means to an end. Her ultimate focus is on engineering a Larkhall wedding. Helen is disinclined to grant permission for the ceremony; Zandra is a known drug-user, to whom she owes no favours. However, she is impressed to hear that Zandra has been clean for three days. A deal is struck: if Zandra successfully completes the prison's detox programme, Helen will consider putting in a good word with the Governing Governor. Zandra is elated, Robin is lukewarm and the two Julies are gifted a project: making the wedding dress.

Small things can become disproportionately important in prison, and Shell is busy exploiting her position in the servery. Rachel finds herself receiving a paltry portion at dinner but summons the strength in Fenner's presence to request more. Shell is canny enough to oblige, not wanting to be too public in her vendetta. Shell is well practiced in the game of cat and mouse.

Further down the servery queue, Nikki bumps into Helen and is dismissive of Helen's attempts at conversation. Fenner, never one to pass up an opportunity to indulge in a little Nikki-baiting, barks that she should show respect for the Wing Governor. Far from being grateful, Helen is frosty to Jim's interference. Nikki can't help but warm to Helen as she publicly chastises Fenner. Could she have got Helen wrong?

Meanwhile, Jim's life is becoming more and more complicated. Due to deliberately dropped remarks from Nikki, his bits on the side now know about each other. Both could expose him: Rachel through naivety and Shell through vengeance. Helen spots Fenner having a cosy chat with Shell in the canteen, and starts to question his professional conduct. His explanation only serves to fuel Helen's suspicions, although she still gets no confirmation from Nikki.

Crystal Gordon, a devout Christian, is moved into Zandra's dorm and is shocked at the prolific drug-taking in the prison. She spits at Helen: 'This ain't a prison, it's a circus and you and your guards are the clowns'. Helen can only privately rue how close Crystal is to the truth.

Zandra has managed to stay off drugs despite chronic withdrawal symptoms and the temptations presented by a Wing full of users and suppliers. As her wedding day draws nearer and Zandra's excitement mounts, Monica Lindsay spots a worrying notice in the newspaper.

Zandra is proudly modelling her wedding dress when she is summoned to Helen's office. She is not prepared for the reason she has been called. Helen must break the news that Robin's family has announced in the papers that he's engaged to another woman. Helen calls Robin into Larkhall to confront a disbelieving Zandra. She is scathing of Robin's explanation that family pressure has forced him to marry someone else. Zandra understands only enough to launch at him and stab him with Helen's pen.

Back in her cell, only Crystal tries to offer Zandra any comfort, telling her that she doesn't need a man to fulfil her dreams. Her alternative is too spiritual for Zandra to contemplate. Besides, she is not as alone as she appears: she is carrying Robin's baby.

EPISODE 4 SERIES 1

Zandra has managed to convince Helen that she wants an abortion. Overwhelmed by Robin's desertion, she is stuck in jail with no prospects and no future. Helen concedes that she is probably doing the right thing, although she remains troubled by Zandra's motives.

Handcuffed to Lorna and Dominic, Zandra is escorted to the clinic. Once there, she capitalises on their empathy by feigning distress at the termination. Lorna goes in search of a nurse, leaving Dom guarding the door. Zandra seizes the opportunity and escapes – her aim is to find Robin and win him back. When she reaches Robin's parental home, she realises her efforts are in vain: Robin is frosty and his mother is positively hostile. Even her shock revelation that she's carrying Robin's child fails to melt Robin's heart or prick his conscience.

At the clinic, Lorna and Dominic are frantic over Zandra's disappearance. After too long a delay, Dominic insists that they must contact Larkhall and admit they've allowed Zandra to escape. Lorna is devastated at the possible consequences for her career. Just as Dominic dials, a dejected and wretched Zandra slumps back into the clinic.

As the relieved prison officers accompany Zandra, still carrying her unborn baby, back to Larkhall, Lorna hatches a plan. She proposes that they keep quiet about Zandra's escape. It would mean two months loss of remission on Zandra's part and possibly dismissal on theirs. Dominic is not convinced: Zandra is a junkie, not someone to trust with such an explosive secret.

Back at Larkhall, Shell and Denny increase their harassment of Rachel. Shell is determined to make Rachel suffer for having an affair with her man, Fenner. Peeling down the photograph of Rachel's baby from her pin board, she cruelly gouges out its eyes. She delivers her threat: either Rachel arranges for her mother to smuggle in a drugs package or she'll harm her child.

Rachel phones her mum to try and persuade her to bring in an 'innocent' package, but to no avail. At visiting time, a suspicious Mrs Hicks arrives empty-handed. Rachel's mind races with the ramifications she will face from Shell. Her mother then delivers a second bombshell – there is something else she hasn't brought with her. Rachel blinks in disbelief as she is told that her mother has placed her ten-month-old daughter into care. Rachel storms from the visiting room.

Back on the Wing, there is no relief from Rachel's torment. After Shell 'accidentally' scalds her with tea, Rachel finds that her one supporter, Jim, has become tired of her emotional dependency. He dismisses her accusations that Shell is trying to kill her, warning

her not to make enemies on the Wing, especially ones as powerful as Shell. Rachel realises that Jim is not her knight in shining armour and that she has been used. She threatens to reveal the whole sordid tale to the Wing Governor. Jim warns her that this would not be very wise.

Monica finds Nikki in silent contemplation in her cell. As resigned tears fall, Nikki confides that her long-standing girlfriend, Trish, has just visited her and ended their relationship. Nikki reveals that Trish is the reason why she is in jail. Her life sentence is for killing the policeman who was trying to rape Trish in the nightclub they owned together. As she recounts the events, her mind becomes determined: she will cope now the way she has always coped. Alone.

Even after lock-up, Rachel cannot escape the constant torment and taunts from her neighbour Shell. In a bid to escape to the 'safety' of solitary confinement, Rachel trashes her cell.

In Helen's office, Rachel will not provide an explanation for her behaviour. Fenner, watching his own back, makes a timely interception. Dressing self-interest as concern, he attributes her breakdown to hearing the news that her baby's been taken into care. In view of this, Helen determines to be lenient. Rachel will not be put on segregation, but she will lose her enhanced status and return to the four-bed dorm. Rachel's head begins to spin: this was the last outcome she wanted.

By nightfall, Rachel's weeping infuriates Denny who, leaping off her bunk, kicks her hard in the stomach. Not satisfied, she later passes Rachel a drawing from Shell depicting a mutilated Rachel. Unable to sleep, Rachel nurses this picture along with the spoiled photograph of her daughter. Her eyes glaze in a moment of clarity. She makes a fatal decision. When Zandra wakes the next morning, it is to see the limp figure of Rachel hanging beside her from the bars on the window.

While the staff are left to orchestrate a formal enquiry, the inmates catcall to each other their crude reactions through the darkness after lights out. Crystal implores them all to respect Rachel's memory and then, into the darkness of the prison yard, she sings her tribute, 'Amazing Grace'. The melody cuts through the noise and replaces it with a deep, pervasive melancholy.

EPISODE 5 SERIES 1

As the shock of Rachel's suicide spreads, her cell is already being cleared for the next inmate. Some at Larkhall are searching their souls to understand the tragedy. Others, who know the real truth are busy covering their tracks. Regardless of the conjecture, Jim is keen to establish that the buck stops with Wing Governor Helen Stewart.

Denny, the weakest link of the conspirators, shows signs that her bravado is cracking and that she fears someone will discover they bullied Rachel. Shell remains unrepentant, announcing tastelessly as she serves up breakfast: 'At least there's an extra helping today'. Nikki is incensed by Shell's lack of contrition and launches at her. Nikki, kicking and screaming, is wrenched away and sent to the block to stew over the injustice.

Meanwhile, Helen and Jim face the music in Stubberfield's office. Jim is keen to plead his defence first. He surmises that Rachel Hicks killed herself because her baby had been taken into care. Simon asks Helen why she didn't put Rachel on suicide-watch, and scoffs at her reply that she didn't consider Rachel a risk. Simon signals that his sympathies are with Jim, saying to Helen: 'I take it you're not a mother'. Simon insists that Helen accepts Fenner's help when facing Rachel's mother, Mrs Hicks – unless of course she has a problem with Jim... Helen, like Nikki, is left seething.

The shock of Rachel's death has provided an adequate excuse for Zandra to bury her good intentions of getting clean from drugs. Dr 'No-No' Nicholson has characteristically refused to prescribe anything for her 'nerves'. She resolves to investigate other, more underhand, strategies.

Helen is forced to meet Mrs Hicks with Fenner acting as minder. Jim manages to make Helen seem like an unfeeling bureaucrat in contrast to his sympathetic words. But Mrs Hicks reveals that Rachel had asked her to collect a package for a prisoner called Shell. Jim's offer to investigate this is all too hasty and Helen, sensing Jim's discomfort, insists on questioning Shell herself. Shell, however, lies, claiming that Rachel begged her to

provide a drugs contact. Helen is unconvinced: the key players in the suicide are slowly becoming apparent.

Zandra has formulated a devastating plan to procure drugs: blackmail. She asks Dominic and Lorna to intervene on her behalf with Dr 'No-No' Nicholson. When both refuse, she threatens to disclose that they covered up her escape from the clinic. Dominic knows that the game is up. Disillusioned and seeing no way out, he contemplates leaving the service. Lorna, kidding herself that she can control the situation, agrees to help out – just this once. Zandra knows that once will not be enough.

Nikki's informal adjudication for fighting with Shell begins badly. Nikki is scornful of Helen's naive determination to make a difference, while Helen is frustrated by Nikki's stubborn refusal to follow the rules. Helen suggests Nikki's behaviour is connected with the break-up of her relationship with Trish. The reply is disparaging: 'You probably don't think it's for real 'cos we're dykes'. Helen is exasperated but sticks to her unorthodox plan. Nikki is surprised but quietly grateful to learn that she is being let off with a warning. Fenner and Hollamby are outraged: this isn't the first time that Helen has dealt favourably with known troublemaker Nikki Wade.

Helen is determined to find answers and visits Rachel's old four-bed dorm – the scene of her suicide. Crystal is more concerned with God's retribution than with Denny's, and recounts the bullying inflicted on Rachel. Rachel wanted solitary confinement to escape from Denny and her tormentors. An irate Helen sends Denny to the punishment block. Denny realises that she is set to take the heat for Rachel's death.

Fearing that Denny may squeal, Jim visits her in solitary and insists that she stick with the story: that Rachel killed herself because she lost her baby. Denny grudgingly obeys and absorbs Helen's wrath at the adjudication. Sentenced to seven days on the block, Denny is

losing her nerve. Why should she take the rap alone? She spills the beans to Helen – Fenner was shagging Rachel. Helen knows she'd need more than Denny's wild allegations to bring Fenner down. The accusation, however, has only served to fuel Helen's private suspicions about Jim.

Helen approaches her tentative confidante, Nikki Wade. Nikki is reluctant to grass but does admit to having warned Rachel off Fenner. This is enough for Helen and, when she confronts Jim, it is clear that her line of questioning ruffles his feathers. He cautions Helen that he'll 'have her' if she repeats her accusation to anyone. But Helen knows he's under pressure: 'Don't threaten me, Jim. It makes you sound guilty'. Helen, for once, has the upper hand.

Helen's triumph is short-lived; when she communicates the development to Stubberfield, she finds that Jim has beaten her to it and reported Helen's allegations to the Governor. Simon has already taken Jim's side. He accuses Helen of having no evidence, no judgement and a questionable ability to do her job. Helen leaves, frustrated and humiliated. Jim has won yet again.

EPISODE 6 **SERIES 1**

As a new group of inmates arrives at Larkhall, there is one, Jessie Devlin, who seems especially dazed and disorientated. Dominic discovers that she is an alcoholic, sentenced for two weeks, and escorts her to the medical wing. As he goes to shut the cell door, she panics: she doesn't want to be left alone. And more specifically, she doesn't want to be left alone without a drink. Dominic is left to wonder at the value of locking up someone who is sick, not a criminal, and this reaffirms his decision to leave the service. When Jessie is left alone in her cell, she collapses with an attack of delirium tremens. Her screams are absorbed by the thin mattress and thick walls.

Helen playfully colludes with Nikki by agreeing to lend her a novel. Recognising Nikki's love of literature, she suggests the inmate follow an Open University course. Nikki derides the notion. Helen, with a hint of flirtation, requests that Nikki at least consider it – as a favour to her. The proposition and its delivery clearly hold some appeal for Nikki.

Shell is manning the lunch counter and cannot resist tormenting Jessie, who has now been moved to the Wing. Jessie hasn't the fortitude to reject the food that Shell spits in. When she drops her cutlery, Bodybag condescendingly instructs her to pick it up, soliciting laughs from the other women. Jessie is degraded as she slumps to her knees. Helen intervenes and makes an indignant Sylvia fetch Jessie a cup of tea. As she helps Jessie back up, Helen's eyes meet Nikki's, who smiles approvingly.

Helen takes Dominic to the pub to persuade him to retract his resignation. He is one of the few officers who treat the women with respect, and they in turn respect him. He is flattered but feels obliged to confess the abortion-clinic debacle with Zandra. Helen, while furious at their stupidity, promises to put in a good word for both officers with the Governing Governor. Lorna, unaware of this development, brings in her mother's Valium for Zandra. Worse, Shell overhears Zandra blackmailing Lorna and wants in on the deal.

Denny shows an unusually benevolent interest in Jessie, and helps to protect her from Shell's taunts. When Jessie divulges that she has no children, Denny is unaccountably upset. Egged on by Shell, she later snaps and marches over to Jessie, pinning her down at knifepoint. Helen, interrogating her in Jessie's presence, can elicit no reason for the assault: it seems to be that Denny is just up to her old tricks. As Jessie repeatedly denies comprehension, Denny blurts out that Jessie is in fact her mother.

Helen has briefed Stubberfield on her officers' cover up of an escape attempt. They agree that Dominic and Lorna should not be formally disciplined but that, instead, Helen will read them the riot act. When Dominic informs Lorna that it is all out in the open, she is only partially relieved. Clear of one transgression, she is now guilty of a far more serious offence.

Jessie is horrified when Shell publicly exposes Denny's abusive childhood. After Jessie gave her up to the social services, she was shipped from one foster home to another. By eleven years old, she was being repeatedly raped by her so-called guardian. By the age of thirteen, she'd had an abortion. 'What sort of mother does that to her kid?' Shell scornfully challenges Jessie. Zandra articulates the hatred of the other women: she spits in Jessie's face.

As the rest of the women turn their backs on Jessie, Nikki reaches out to her. Jessie heeds Nikki's advice to write Denny a letter explaining why she put her into care. Denny initially rejects the gesture. Jessie pleads with her to read it. Frustrated, and with tears streaming down her face, she screams at Jessie that she 'can't bloody read'.

Zandra helps by reading the letter to Denny. In it, Jessie explains that she herself suffered years of abuse and turned to the bottle. She had lived for drink, not for her child, and had not been the mother that Denny deserved. When they took Denny away, she was convinced that it would be to a better life. Denny, on hearing the heartfelt apology, crumples sobbing into Zandra's arms.

Helen finds Nikki in the library reading *Romeo and Juliet*. Nikki, smiling, admits that Juliet and Juliet is more her cup of tea. Helen asks Nikki how she knows she isn't interested in men. Nikki replies: 'The same way as you are – if you are'. Helen laughs

uncomfortably: 'I'm not interested in women – not in that way'. Nikki leaves the room with the memorable parting words: 'You should try it some time. You don't know what you're missing'.

Now that Denny has found her mum, she doesn't want to lose her. She plans to break out when Jessie is due for release. Jessie insists she will visit, but Denny doesn't believe her. Jessie tries to explain that, as an alcoholic, she wouldn't have enough to offer Denny and, besides, Denny would be caught and end up spending more time inside. Denny is devastated and takes it as the final rejection. Having given up hope, Denny is ecstatic some days later to receive a postcard from Jessie asking for a visiting order. Jessie also proudly declares: 'so far so good'. She hasn't had a drink since her release.

EPISODE 7 SERIES 1

Helen's day starts with a surprise – a proposal from Sean. He teases her that her maternal instincts are wasted on the prisoners and that the time has come to make an honest woman of her. Helen is distinctly cool and hastily excuses herself for work. They will discuss it later, but yes, of course she loves him.

Zandra, by now heavily pregnant, has continued to escape into her own private drug-induced abyss. Shell and Denny are only jealous of her seemingly endless supply of jellies. In the dorm, they get Crystal to leave the cell by pretending they are determined to confiscate Zandra's stash for her own protection. A cynical Crystal leaves, believing that the end will justify the means. Actually, Crystal couldn't begin to guess their agenda; shaking Zandra from her stupor, Shell informs her she has found out about her little blackmail scam with Lorna Rose. Naturally she wants in.

Under Shell's instruction, Zandra demands a private conference with Lorna. Following her into the bathroom, Lorna mistakenly believes she has the upper hand. Triumphantly she explains she no longer needs to be threatened by Zandra. Her bosses now know about the escape attempt she and Dominic covered up. Zandra doesn't seem overly concerned by this revelation. A toilet flushes and Shell strides out of the cubicle. She is now a witness. Shell scoffs: it's not the cover-up they'll tell about – it's the supplying of drugs. That's if Lorna is stupid enough not to bring any more in.

At the daily prison officers' meeting, Helen proposes that, in the light of Nikki's improved behaviour, she should be rewarded with a move to Enhanced. Jim and Sylvia are aghast. It is left to an indignant Sylvia to

impart the 'good news'. Nikki is astounded, but not too stunned to cheek Bodybag who curtly informs her that she wouldn't have been so foolhardy as to confer special treatment on her. The decision was the Governor's.

Prison-issue plastic bag in hand, Nikki ascends to G3. Her new neighbour, Shell, is outraged and demands an explanation. Nikki is deadpan in her response: the move was the Governor's idea. 'You must be shagging her,' Shell charges. Nikki ignores the jibe but it's clearly not a notion that displeases her. Shell's attempts to provoke a fight with Nikki fail; Nikki, realising it's a crass ploy to get her in trouble and off Enhanced, gallantly restrains her temper. Helen has stuck her neck out for her and she has no intention of letting her down.

Sean has been press-ganged by Helen into giving a gardening lecture to the women.

Nikki, clueless as to his identity, comes to his rescue when Shell and Denny heckle. But Nikki's helpfulness comes to an abrupt end when Sean reveals that he is Helen's fiancé. 'You learn something new every day,' Nikki barbs, before she sharply exits.

Helen finds Nikki in the potting shed and demands that she account for her evident distress at the news of her engagement. Nikki scoffs at what she sees as feigned innocence: 'You want to know what this is about? It's about this'. Grabbing Helen's hand, she raises it to her breast. Helen balks and, hurriedly composing herself, turns tail and leaves.

Dominic, spying the constant traffic in and out of Shell's cell, correctly suspects drug-dealing. He drags a terror-stricken Lorna along for an impromptu search. She doesn't need to inspect the cell to know what a search will uncover. And the bounty will have come courtesy of her.

Dominic is on the verge of grudgingly conceding defeat. He cautions Shell that this is lucky for her, when Charlie, her canary, catches his eye. Dominic searches its cage and, nestling in the bird food, are a couple of bright blue jellies. Shell protests vehemently: Nikki Wade must have planted them there. She demands to see her personal officer, Jim Fenner. Jim is called from the P.O.'s office and is furious, how dare she summon him? In a tight corner, Shell tells him about Lorna Rose. This only adds to Jim's fury, and he asks how she can dare to lie about a fellow officer. Jim violently pushes Shell to the floor. She is on her own now.

Helen and Nikki are both having a hard time coming to terms with the incident in the shed. Helen orders Nikki to her office to make clear that it must never happen again. Helen forcefully states that she is not a lesbian and that Nikki must find another object of her affections: 'Nikki, even if I were attracted to you, which I'm not, there is no way we could have a relationship. For a start, I would be sacked.' Nikki senses that Helen's wrath is partially borne out of the knowledge that the attraction is reciprocated. Helen, though, is implacable and Nikki sarcastically apologises for having caused the Wing Governor so much trouble. Sean is blissfully unaware that some of Helen's renewed ardour that night could be attributed to overcompensation.

As Nikki, up on the 3s, reels from Helen's rejection, Shell spends her first night back on Basic following her drugs bust. Without Fenner's support, she is no longer queen of the landings. Shell feels humiliated and swears revenge on Lorna. In a silent rage, she contents herself by destroying the other participant in her downfall: she flushes her canary, Charlie, down the loo.

EPISODE 8 | SERIES 1

Shell threatens that she will withdraw privileges from Fenner until he gets her back on Enhanced. The Julies meanwhile have discovered their own antidote to 'Larkhall blues': Julie Saunders' son, David, has sent her thinly veiled instructions in the art of home brewing. Following a chat with Monica, they realise that Chateau Larkhall is within their grasp. Monica is not blessed with such good news. Helen informs her that her home visit with Spencer has been delayed. Monica consoles herself that she will now have time to finish the jumper she is knitting for him.

The Julies do have one problem to overcome in their quest for hooch: where to keep it. They approach an unenthusiastic Nikki to ask if they can use the potting shed. She asks for starters how they will keep it warm. 'We'll take turns to come out and hug it,' Julie J. replies, bright-eyed. But Nikki, spying the compost heap, has a better idea. She accepts the sterilising tablets, courtesy of the mother and baby unit, and prepares her watering can.

Nikki and Julie S. hurriedly prepare the wine for fermentation. However, Julie J. proves

conspicuous as a lookout and Bodybag's suspicions are aroused. She demands entry to the shed. Nikki hears the disturbance and reacts quickly, whipping off her top in front of a surprised Julie S. The door is wrenched open to reveal the two women in their bras, caught, apparently, in flagrante delicto. Bodybag is disgusted: 'You turn my stomach, your sort'. But the hooch has remained a secret.

Monica is summoned to Helen's office where she receives terrible news: Spencer has died of a heart attack in the early hours. Helen's words of comfort are met with derision: 'You know nothing about me, nothing about my life – none of you, you know nothing!' The only help Helen can offer is of a practical nature, supporting Monica back to her cell, providing sedation and cradling her until she falls asleep. She tells the other officers to watch her closely and treat her with utmost respect, granting all reasonable requests.

Helen seeks Nikki and solace. Instead, Nikki merely grills Helen as to how she can go home while Monica is stuck in jail miles from her son's body. Defensive, Helen abruptly terminates their discussion 'I didn't come here for a debate'. As she walks back down the landing Nikki's jibes of her being 'just like the rest of them' ring in her ears. Helen finds even less comfort outside Larkhall. Sean is preoccupied with organising their impending wedding.

The prisoners, discovering Monica's loss, try to rally to her aid. She has descended into a state of inertia and is uncommunicative. The Julies, at a loss as to how to show their support, promise to crack open the alcohol for a wake in tribute to Spencer. Even Nikki cannot break through to Monica, who retreats far into herself, clasping Spencer's unfinished and redundant jumper. She is overwhelmed by her loss and her sense of guilt: she should have been there.

The day of the funeral arrives and Helen escorts a numb, impassive Monica to the church, having reluctantly handcuffed her. In the service, Helen allows her judgement to override regulations and slips off the cuffs. It is the most real way that she can show her respect for the older woman. At the graveside, Monica watches in growing anguish as the first handfuls of dirt are thrown on to the coffin. Her grief finally hits her and she climbs into the grave to follow her son. She chants her mantra to him: she will stay with him always.

Back on G-Wing, Shell informs Fenner that Nikki is brewing alcohol in the potting shed. Fenner is delighted: this could get Wade out of his hair and out of his prison for good. Fenner overturns the shed for evidence. Nikki allows herself a smug smile in the direction of the compost heap where the wine is concealed and fermenting nicely. Fenner is livid with Shell when the search for the alcohol is unsuccessful. As far as he is concerned, she can rot on Basic.

The hooch is raised on a swinger and dispensed into the Julies' sink. The wake commences, despite the fact that Monica has not yet returned. Chateau Larkhall proves rough but potent. Before long, sounds of merriment are echoing around the walls of the wing. Sylvia bursts into the cell but finds them all deep in prayer, the hooch having been flushed. Denny has the hiccups but nothing can be proved. 'Wake my backside,' Sylvia grumbles, breaking up the party.

When Monica arrives back on the wing, Helen pauses outside Nikki's cell, telling her that Monica needs some time alone. She pauses before adding that she does too. Nikki remarks, with a little bitterness, that she has Sean to go home to. Unspoken words flow through the cell door that separates them, but they only wish each other goodnight.

After lock-up, the women shout words of commiseration and support to Monica, but she blanks them out. Instead, she sings quietly through tears to her solitary photo of Spencer.

EPISODE 9 SERIES 1

The prisoners revel in the memory of Chateau Larkhall, if not in the taste of it. Crystal is not amused: 'If the papers knew what went on here it would be a scandal,' she declares. Shell is the only one to agree. In fact, Shell seems to have turned over a new leaf. She assures an indignant Zandra and suspicious Lorna that there will be no more blackmailing. Fenner is also perturbed by her strange behaviour. 'I'm thinking of changing my ways, if you must know,' she replies evenly. She pronounces that she is giving up drugs and taking up religion. 'The nearest you'll get to religion is the missionary position,' Jim dismisses.

Helen clears the remnants of another night spent seeking solace in a vodka bottle. Sean is equally self-absorbed, focusing on their imminent wedding. Helen's home life seems to be becoming almost as stressful as her professional one.

Crystal cautiously accepts the sincerity of Shell's reform and is inspired by her suggestion to write to the newspapers, outlining the drug epidemic on G-Wing. For good measure, she hands Shell her Bible and invites her to the chapel for worship. The other prisoners can only debate the plausibility of Shell being part of the 'God squad'.

Helen searches for Monica but instead finds Nikki. The tension between them is palpable. Nikki is brazen and pushes Helen to confess her true feelings. Helen hisses: 'This is difficult for me, as I think you know!' 'So what *do* you want?' Nikki asks. But this is a question that Helen can't yet answer for herself.

Helen is dismayed when she overhears Monica call off her appeal. Monica refuses to listen to reason: 'There's nothing for me out there anymore. I want to forget the life I've had. Being in here helps me do that – numbs the brain.' Helen falls back on Nikki to change her mind. Perhaps Nikki can have some success as a friend where Helen has failed as an officer.

Nikki duly pays Monica a visit to convince her to keep up with her appeal, but she finds her unyielding. Eventually, Monica concedes that she is being hasty and will reconsider. Nikki is relieved; she'll have some welcome news for Helen. Nikki is unaware that Monica's turnaround has less to do with a genuine change of heart and more to do with preventing Nikki from uncovering her secret. When Nikki departs, Monica returns to counting her hoard of pills. She has decided on a different way out of Larkhall from an appeal.

Helen is stunned by the news that a letter of Crystal's has been published in the *Guardian*; she had tried to talk to her about the drug situation. She is immediately summoned to Simon Stubberfield's office. Simon is quick to displace the blame from his door to hers. Her defence that drugs are rife in every prison is ignored. The letter was about G-Wing and, as Governor, Helen is to take the fallout.

On the Wing, Crystal discovers that her letter has not been favourably received. The two Julies are furious, believing that it will lead to closed visits. As they fume at Crystal, Shell and Denny look on, laughing. Could Crystal have been used as a patsy?

Shell has one last favour to ask of the long-suffering Lorna. Shell's mother has a bottle of perfume for her, which she would like Lorna to smuggle in. Lorna is reluctant but agrees. When the perfume is delivered, she examines the packaging to ensure that she is not inadvertently delivering any other contraband. It seems to be all clear.

Shell asks Crystal to accompany her to Helen's office, to blow the whistle on a corrupt, drug-dealing screw. Helen is sceptical but she can't ignore the accusation. Staking out the landing that night, she catches Lorna in the act. Shell is self-satisfied, Lorna is horrified and Helen detects a setup. A meticulous examination of the box, by the DST, reveals a bag of white powder nestling between the layers of cardboard. In the time it takes to say 'It's a lucky bag, all right', Lorna is ushered from Larkhall by the police.

For once, Stubberfield is sanguine; Helen has made demonstrable progress in the fight against drugs. Nevertheless, despite her objections, he orders closed visits to finally stem the drug problem. Helen returns home in despair, uncertain that she can face another day

on G-Wing. Sean's reassurance that the wedding preparations are going well is small comfort.

Amid the tension, a new arrival is escorted onto the Wing. 'The name's Yvonne. Hope you like a good party, girls,' she quips. She is a gangland wife and it's clear that her influence outside will ensure she's a formidable force inside too. Denny is impressed. Shell, sensing competition, is not.

Finding no comfort at home or amongst her staff, Helen finally seeks out Nikki. 'I'm just getting it on both sides, Nikki,' she sobs, 'From above, and below...' Nikki's comforting caresses suddenly turn into a tender kiss. Helen responds until her senses return and she abruptly springs from the bed. Nikki is immediately remorseful: 'I shouldn't have done that!' she laments. 'No you shouldn't,' Helen snaps. As she traces her shaking fingers on the lips that Nikki has just kissed, Helen knows she has crossed a line.

EPISODE 10 SERIES 1

Shell finds herself ostracised on the Wing just as new inmate Yvonne Atkins is becoming increasingly popular. The women are irate at the imposition of closed visits and blame Shell and Crystal for setting up Lorna Rose. Shell discards her religious façade, realising no one takes it seriously. She curtly rebuffs Crystal's invitation to go and pray. Her next move is to apologise to Jim in a way he'll understand. She needs his patronage on the Wing but she'll still get her revenge. She writes an anonymous letter to his wife exposing their affair.

Helen has avoided Nikki since their kiss. Unable to stall an inevitable meeting, she

summons the despondent prisoner to her office. Helen accuses Nikki of taking advantage of her and reinforces that her interest is purely professional. Nikki doesn't buy it but is silenced when Helen plaintively insists that one of them will have to leave Larkhall if Nikki's infatuation continues.

Yvonne spots that, under arcane prison rules, every inmate is allowed a guitar. She promptly arranges for twelve guitars to be delivered and the Larkhall Tabernacle Gospel Choir is born. They will keep playing – badly – until the screws sign their petition to reinstate open visits. Despite Helen's warnings to Yvonne that her wealth and influence on the outside mean nothing inside, clearly she is a force to be reckoned with. Shell is far from happy about Atkins usurping her position as top dog and attempts to threaten her. Yvonne is unimpressed with her show of bravado: 'I don't do scared.'

Monica is continuing with the pretence that she intends to go through with her appeal, which is scheduled for the next day. Privately, she is still hoarding her anti-depression pills and has traded phone cards for alcohol miniatures to wash the pills down with. Nikki becomes suspicious of Monica's odd behaviour. As she interrogates her, Monica slumps onto the bed, saying: 'You're too late, Nikki'.

Crystal is counting the choir into their first practice run of 'Kumbaya': 'one, two, three, four...' Meanwhile, Nikki and the two Julies are also counting aloud as they force Monica to keep walking up and down her tiny cell: 'one, two, three, four...' They force cold coffee down her throat in an effort to conquer the effects of her overdose. Monica doesn't respond.

Bodybag's nerves are starting to fray at the choir's racket. As Yvonne informs the women to keep practising after lock-up, Crystal announces that the noise will stop when Sylvia signs the petition. Sylvia grunts.

The Julies can't understand why Nikki hasn't called in the medics yet; Monica is slipping away. Nikki gives it one more go – more cold coffee and pacing. Just as she is about to give in and sound the alarm, Monica starts to retch. As she is violently sick, her friends are filled with relief.

Helen, checking on Monica in her cell, is immediately suspicious. She quizzes Nikki who confirms that Monica took an overdose. Helen is incensed and questions how Nikki could be so irresponsible as to not get a doctor. Nikki knows that Helen can't survive another prison scandal: 'I did it to protect you'.

Bodybag waits until no one is watching, storms across the Wing and opens a cell hatch. 'Where's that petition?' Round one: Yvonne.

The next morning, Monica apologises to Nikki. Nikki is blunt, telling her she should feel ashamed of herself. Most of the other women she'll be leaving behind are without hope, their whole lives wasted. 'When someone like you comes along and says that they'd rather be dead than free? I'm sorry, but everyone who gets out of here gets out for all of us.' Monica is humbled. Helen thanks Nikki for her help, even if she can't condone her methods. Nikki, tired of the hypocrisy, tells her not to bother.

G-Wing assembles around the communal television to watch reports of Monica's appeal. The newscaster confirms her release and screams of joy echo around the Wing. Monica proceeds to make a statement which resonates with the prisoners. She has learnt that women in prison are not monsters or lunatics but usually victims of abusive men, drugs and a system that incarcerates, bullies and dehumanises them. Many will lose their families – some, like her, forever. They need help and support, which is precisely what those same prisoners gave her and how she survived. She emotionally concludes: 'In my opinion, prison, as punishment, only makes bad situations worse'.

Helen must also act on recent lessons. She is in turmoil as she meets Sean, who is trying on his suit for the wedding. She explains that she can't marry him: she doesn't love him. She makes a tearful departure back to her anchor – her work at the prison.

As the women stage an impromptu party on the Wing, Sean arrives at the prison. In the garden, he erects a stake and hangs his now redundant wedding suit on it. Just as Helen approaches him, he sets the suit alight before coldly throwing her house keys back at her. The women gather at the window to witness the humiliating spectacle. They shout their support to the Wing Governor. Jim is quietly delighted; he's on the up once more. As Helen leaves the prison, she looks back and catches Nikki's unmistakable concern.

Order on the Wing is restored and the women are locked up for another night. Helen returns home to an empty house and an empty love life. Nikki permits herself a smile. Now that Sean is out of the picture, she is ready to fill the void.

No Giggling: Continuity Shots

Lindsey Fawcett, who plays Shaz Wylie, explains how essential these are to the filming of Bad Girls.

Our filming is done in blocks of two or three episodes, all filmed simultaneously. This means that we film scenes from the episodes in any order, which can become quite confusing. That's where 'continuity shots' come into play; after each take used (i.e. when no one fluffs a line, or giggles, or accidentally says the 'f' word!), someone from Make-up and someone from Wardrobe takes a Polaroid of each actor in the scene.

The next time we film a scene from that particular 'day' in Larkhall (which might be up to two weeks later), Make-up and Wardrobe can look at the Polaroids and know exactly what we should be wearing and exactly how many strands of hair were hanging down where.

On a typical day, we may have up to twenty or so Polaroids taken of us. This would become boring if it weren't for the fact that so many of us pull ridiculous faces. We thought you might be interested to see the *Bad Girls* doing what they do best … being bad! Enjoy.

EPISODE 1 SERIES 2

Nikki is miserable. Helen hasn't returned to Larkhall since her dramatic break-up with Sean. Fenner, conversely, is euphoric. Helen's absence has cleared the way for a career coup. His role as acting Wing Governor is set to become permanent. Jim's wife, Marilyn, is too preoccupied to care: she has been receiving anonymous notes informing her of her husband's affair with one Shell Dockley.

On G-Wing, Zandra goes into labour and is whisked off to hospital. She is accompanied by Dominic and an ever-truculent Sylvia, who insists that the baby's father won't show: 'If your boyfriend was remotely interested in this baby he wouldn't have married someone else, would he?'

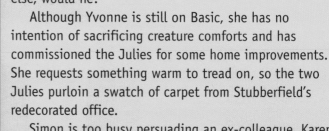

Although Yvonne is still on Basic, she has no intention of sacrificing creature comforts and has commissioned the Julies for some home improvements. She requests something warm to tread on, so the two Julies purloin a swatch of carpet from Stubberfield's redecorated office.

Simon is too busy persuading an ex-colleague, Karen Betts, to consider a position at Larkhall to notice the theft. Jim joins the reception committee, and it is clear that no introductions are necessary. Karen is unsentimental at seeing her old fling again: 'You've put on weight, Jim,' she remarks dryly.

Zandra gives birth to a baby boy and even Sylvia becomes caught up in the special moment. Robin does eventually arrive, enthused at the birth, and Zandra discovers he didn't go through with his marriage so there is still a chance for them. However, when the nurse informs them that the baby is withdrawing from the drugs Zandra has been taking, she is devastated and Robin is furious.

Jim's dreams of life as a 'suit' are dissipated when he arrives at work to find Helen has re-established herself in the Wing Governor's office. Her absence was due to a delayed flight. Simon is unimpressed, issuing her with an official warning, telling her that Fenner is to remain on the same grade and that a new principal officer is to be appointed in an effort to ensure a strong team on G-Wing.

Helen enters the servery to announce the news of Zandra's birth, to be greeted with jubilation by the women at her return. Nikki is especially delighted but, when she is summoned to Helen's office later, things do not go to plan. Helen tells her that the relationship with Sean was never going to work, dispelling Nikki's impression that she had been a factor in the break-up. Helen does admit that Nikki means something to her but, as long as she is charged with locking Nikki up, they can never have a relationship: 'How can I do my job when I'm breaking my own rules? I'm sorry, Nikki, but there's no way.' Nikki retaliates, saying: 'Well you obviously care more about your bloody career than you do about me.' Helen concedes that she does need Nikki; she is on her last chance at Larkhall and needs help in making things better. Nikki is incredulous that favours are being asked of her under the circumstances and walks off.

Jim tells Shell about the letters. Shell is initially terrified that she has been rumbled, but is relieved when Jim points to Nikki as his chief suspect. She presses him for details of Marilyn's reaction and is disappointed to learn that Fenner's wife is prepared to believe his word over that of a con. It is time for Shell to pick up the pace. Paper and pens are not as effective as direct communications: Shell sets about acquiring a phone.

Zandra soon realises that, even on the mother and baby unit, she is not safe from the temptation of drugs. Despite her determination to stay clean for little Robby, her nerves are soon fraught. She uses a phonecard to buy herself a fix but manages to conquer her craving. The dealer isn't as flexible and a fight erupts. Zandra is hauled in front of Helen and Robin. Her involvement in the drama reinforces his belief that she is an unfit mother. 'You weren't there with me the whole time I was carrying him so you can piss off now!' screams Zandra. Robin reveals that he has already begun legal proceedings for sole custody.

Zandra is determined that no one is going to steal her baby and resorts to desperate measures. She climbs onto the hospital wing roof, where she teeters on the edge clutching her baby wrapped in prison issue sheets. Jim races up to the roof but his attempts to coax Zandra down fail miserably. It is Helen's turn.

Helen ventures out onto the roof edge towards Zandra and the prisoners below watch with baited breath. 'He'll only win if you give up the fight,' Helen tells her. Helen goes on to promise that she'll help protect Zandra's rights as a mother, but implores her to also respect her child's rights. Eventually, and to great cheers from below, Zandra hands Helen

the baby. As soon as she does, she is overcome with despair and prepares to jump. Dominic grabs her just in time.

Nikki calls Helen over, praising her for resolving the crisis: 'I've got to tell you, you're gorgeous,' she states honestly. 'I'm totally in love with you, there's nothing I can do about it.' Helen stiffly replies: 'Well I can.' Nikki, stuck behind the ever-present bars that separate them, can only watch her walk away. Helen does not look back.

EPISODE 2 SERIES 2

Shell continues her vengeful campaign against Fenner with anonymous phone calls to his wife. Jim naturally denies the alleged affair but pledges to uncover the 'hoaxer'. His chief suspect remains Nikki Wade, a wrongful accusation that suits Shell very well indeed.

Karen Betts is establishing herself on the Wing. She admits some trepidation at the prospect of looking after women inmates; women's prisons don't have a reputation for good behaviour. In addition, she is fending off renewed interest from Jim since their brief liaison at a conference four years ago.

Fenner decides that enough is enough and targets Nikki's cell for an unsanctioned spin. Ignoring her protestations of ignorance, he frantically rummages through her possessions, searching for the phone. Nikki snaps when he starts throwing her precious books around,

and she lashes out at Dominic who has come to check up on the commotion. She is hauled kicking and screaming to the punishment block.

Helen is highly suspicious of Jim's motives for searching Nikki's cell but concedes that she must have had something to hide. After all, Nikki did hit Dominic. She seeks Nikki out in the block but, to her dismay, finds her unrepentant. Nikki blames Fenner for provoking her and appeals to Helen to admit that her love is reciprocated. Helen is in deep denial and compensates by refusing to countenance anything Nikki has to say. Nikki snarls back: 'I know I knock Fenner – at

least when he fancies a con, he has the courage to give her one'. Helen steels herself to make a mammoth decision: Nikki is transferred to another prison.

Yvonne has taken a motherly interest in Denny, and is touched when Denny recounts her reunion with her mother. When Jessie waits outside the prison on visiting day, Yvonne arranges the delivery of a birthday present for her – an envelope containing £200. Jessie is startled by the gesture but Denny reassures her it is above board. She suggests Jessie puts it towards a flat so they can share a life together after Denny's release. When Denny excitedly relays this to Yvonne, she confesses that this is the first time in her life she's had something to look forward to.

Shell offers Marilyn the proof she demands. She secretes the phone in her bed sheets so that Marilyn can hear the sordid details of the tryst Shell has arranged with Jim. Devastated by the betrayal, Marilyn promptly arrives at Larkhall to tell Jim not to bother coming home – ever. Enraged, Fenner goes to take his revenge on Nikki Wade. He is stopped in his tracks when Helen informs him that Nikki was shipped out that morning. His face contorts in sudden comprehension. Nikki couldn't have made those calls...but he knows now who did.

As anticipated, Jim discovers the mobile on Shell. He is enraged and beats her up. Karen notices Fenner walking out of the cell, wiping clean his blood-stained hands. Jim is blasé

and lies that Shell was wilfully self-harming. Karen, seeing the bloodied and bruised figure slumped on the floor, is doubtful. She escorts Shell to Helen's office, instructing her to tell the truth.

Helen listens in horror to Shell's story. She accuses Jim of having forced her to have sex for many years but insists that she did not call his wife. She also reveals he was having sex with the tragic Rachel before she committed suicide. To Helen's shock, Shell confirms that Jim suspected Nikki of the phone calls and deliberately wound her up to get her shipped out of Larkhall. Helen is resolved and shamed; Jim will not escape the consequences of his actions and neither will she. She will demand that Simon must at last deal with Jim, but first she calls to arrange for Nikki to be returned to Larkhall. Nikki's sweatbox is turned around to begin the long journey back to Larkhall.

Jim has busied himself with writing up his version of events. Helen doesn't believe him but Simon doesn't need much persuasion to sweep everything under the carpet. Helen, however, insists: 'Either he goes or I go.' Simon reluctantly suspends Jim when Helen threatens to take the case up with area management. Helen angrily realises that Simon is intractable and has only suspended Jim to save his own skin. She is on a roll and unleashes her pent up critique of Simon's management of the prison. He pulls rank and reminds her that he is in charge of Larkhall whether she likes it or not. 'Well I don't like it,' she replies. 'I don't like it one bit.'

Fenner leaves Larkhall with his few belongings, to the accompaniment of catcalls from the women. Helen has an apology to make. She visits Nikki and explains that she let her feelings cloud her professional judgement. She should have listened to Nikki when Nikki claimed Fenner had provoked her. Helen also has news to break: she has resigned. Nikki is aghast but Helen reminds her that, as she is no longer Nikki's jailer, she can at last express her true feelings. She leans forward and gently pulls Nikki into a deep kiss. Nikki withdraws and begs her to at least visit but Helen believes that it would be too difficult. 'This is shit, Helen,' she cries. Gently stroking her face, Helen turns to leave: 'Shit happens,' she offers. Nikki is broken-hearted.

EPISODE 3 | SERIES 2

The morning mail brings surprises for two of the inmates. Denny receives word that her mother plans to visit and Nikki receives an unexpected letter from Helen. The beginning of Jim's day is not so pleasant: he awakes on his sofa to Marilyn snapping: 'I thought I told you not to bother coming home.' He tells her he has been set up, that Shell manipulated him into sex; 'Most men wouldn't last a week inside Larkhall,' he plaintively appeals.

Karen Betts is flattered by the promotion Simon offers. She wants to be Wing Governor, but has reservations. Simon is quick to reassure her, insinuating that all of the Wing's recent problems can be attributed to Helen; of course she will enjoy his full support. Meanwhile, Sylvia is not impressed, 'She'll be out of that uniform and into a suit faster than you can say Clark Kent,' she moans.

Back on the Wing, there is a shock for Julie J. in Yvonne's morning paper. Her ex-husband's father, Eddie 'The Drill' Dawson, has died, which means that her children will be coming over from America to attend the funeral. Julie J. is desperate to see her kids, whom she hasn't seen for years. Julie S. decides to engineer a compassionate license for her to get to the funeral. Rehearsals of fake tears are in vain: Dom explains that you are only allowed out for close relatives.

When Jim's assault on Shell looks likely to go to court, Marilyn grudgingly agrees to help him, if only for the sake of the children. Shell, without the patronage of Jim, has lost her status in the prison and is ecstatic to receive two letters. One is from Marilyn complaining that her marriage is now over – and the other is from Jim, who professes his undying love. Denny suggests that it's just an attempt to get her to drop the allegations but Shell will not hear good advice.

Despite Karen's reservations, and to the relief of Simon, Shell withdraws her accusation. Jim has no case to answer and his career and neck have once again been saved.

Julie J. vents her despair on a bullying Hollamby. Trapped in the confines of her cell, she becomes more and more despondent, causing Julie S. to become concerned enough to explain the situation to Yvonne. If there is one thing Yvonne understands, it is a mother's love and – with a gangland husband – miracles can be worked. One phone call later and her daughter, Lauren, is set up to extract the children from the funeral and bring them to see Julie J. on visiting day.

The big day arrives and Julie J. waits nervously at her table, eyes glued to the door. She is not the only one: Denny is anxiously waiting for her mum who hasn't arrived. Denny tries to invent a reason; she's not prepared to assume the worst. When Julie J.'s two children hesitantly approach their mother, they are uncomfortable and quiet with her. A question has been weighing on their minds. Is she really a prostitute? Julie hesitates. How can she explain that she did what she had to do in order to support them?

Sylvia has fixed her beady eyes on the children talking to Julie. She knows full well that

Julie has a court order preventing contact between mother and children. Amid protestations from prisoners and visitors alike, Hollamby manhandles the bemused children out of the room. Julie J. can only believe she has lost them forever.

'Evil, she is, bloody evil' Julie S. bitterly complains about the officer. But what can they do? She is untouchable. Yvonne smiles: 'I don't know about that. There are ways and means to get back at them.'

Jim Fenner, meanwhile, has one more loose end to tie up before he can relax. In Shell's cell, he manipulates her into surrendering the letter he wrote to her. 'Any more incriminating evidence in here?' he asks as soon as she produces the piece of paper. His tone is suddenly harsh. As he repossesses Marilyn's letter, he reveals that he dictated it. 'Do you really think I'd leave my wife for a little slut like you?' he asks. Shell knows that she cannot report him again: no one will believe her. She has been played for a fool.

When Karen spies Jim leaving Shell's cell, she is suspicious; she knows that Jim has

manipulated his way back into a job. Her requests for Jim to be transferred to another wing have been turned down but she makes no pretence about how she feels about him. 'I don't want you on my wing. I don't trust you,' she tells him, only to be informed smugly that he is staying put. 'In that case, you'd better hang on tight, you're in for a rough ride,' she announces, finally wiping the smile from his face.

He is not the only one. The Julies are working industriously, laying a thick layer of polish on the stairs in line with Yvonne's plan for revenge. Sure enough, when Hollamby stamps up the stairs towards them, she slips and is caught by the extravagantly concerned prisoners. The women surround her and in the confusion that follows, Hollamby is pushed down the stairs, knocking herself unconscious on the hard floor of G1. The women look down without remorse. There are ways and means to get back at them.

EPISODE 4 SERIES 2

There is tension in the officers' room. Sylvia, sporting a neck brace, harps on about the results of the investigation into her fall, while the animosity between Jim and Karen is becoming palpable. Jim has been stripped of his role as Shell's personal officer and the task falls to Dominic. An over-welcoming Shell is waiting for him when he visits her cell: 'Wait! Don't you want me to be your little girl?' Dom makes a speedy exit.

Denny, still reeling from her mother's failure to turn up on visiting day, receives word that Jessie is in hospital following an accident. She is granted temporary release to see her but, on arrival, discovers that Jessie has discharged herself. A swiftly arranged detour to Jessie's hostel is also in vain. Denny's first instinct is to sit and wait. Di, ever-sympathetic, promises that she will help find Jessie, however Denny must return to prison. Denny miserably consents but, as they walk to the taxi rank, Denny spots her mother, blind drunk and cavorting in a park bandstand. Jessie hurls abuse at Denny, saying she has never been anything but trouble. Denny is heartbroken

and tries desperately to reason with her. When Jessie boasts that she spent the money her daughter gave her on drink, Denny throws down the flowers she bought and walks away in disgust.

Jim finds himself allocated to tasks that he considers beneath him and is convinced that Karen is trying to undermine him. He informs Karen he is starting grievance proceedings against her, on grounds of unprofessional conduct. 'You'd know all about that, wouldn't you?' Karen points out, grimly amused. Jim, undeterred, arranges a game of golf with Simon, to 'discuss' things, man to man. Jim 'reluctantly' confesses that he and Karen had a brief fling and suggests that Karen is letting this interfere with her professional judgement. But Simon, for once, has the measure of Jim. He takes the wind out of his sails by informing him that Karen had already told him upon her appointment, just to be professional. Simon advises Jim to cut his losses, be glad he still has a job, and not try to have his cake and eat it. Jim will need a new tack to deal with Karen Betts.

Josh, the civilian prison handyman, has set his sights on a distinctly cool but slowly softening Crystal. His progress is thwarted when Crystal discovers him talking to a flirtatious Shell, unaware that he is rebuffing her advances. Shell, with two seduction failures in one day, is deflated. Karen suggests that she should have learned her lesson with Fenner and not have propositioned Dom. She then poses a question that unnerves

Shell: 'Don't you think you're worth more than that?'
The two Julies do not agree: 'You're nothing but an
evil little slut, Shell Dockley,' they sneer. The words
echo in her mind and, compelled to punish herself,
she sits alone in her cell barely wincing as she stubs
her cigarette out on her hand.

Always delighted by a new project, the Julies
busily plan a surprise for Crystal to reunite her with
Josh. Julie S. has seen future love in Crystal's tea
leaves and, with the help of the other prisoners,
organises a secret candlelit meal for two in the
laundry. As the couple tuck into sausages, mash and
orange squash, the Julies peek through the keyhole
and witness romance blossoming.

Yvonne senses that Denny needs to vent her anger and disappointment after the
incident with her mother. She grabs a mattress and invites Denny to work through her
aggression. Denny pummels it till sated and collapses sobbing into Yvonne's maternal
embrace. Yvonne tells her that she has to start liking and respecting herself before she can
expect others to do the same. When a sober Jessie Devlin appears on the next visiting day
and tries to apologise for her behaviour, she finds her daughter has matured. Jessie has
promised to come off the booze before. Denny calmly tells her that if she is still sober in a
year's time, they can discuss a future together, but she does not want to hear from her until
then. 'Fingers crossed, eh?' Denny sadly smiles before asking to return to her cell.

Jim, smarting from Simon's reproach, informs Karen that he has decided to drop the
grievance procedure. He admits he has made many mistakes but that Karen can see right
through him. She is not surprised at his change of heart: 'Simon gave me a ring last night –
said you'd had a very pleasant game of golf.' Jim accuses Karen of enjoying his discomfort.

She warns him: 'It's not about getting one up on
you, Jim, it's about working with officers I can
trust. The next time you step out of line, I'll be
ready and it won't just be a suspension.'

Jim decides that working within the rules is a
mug's game. Edging up to Yvonne, he suggests a
mutually beneficial deal. He is sure that she
would appreciate a private visiting room with
her husband, in return for which Jim would get
financial renumeration for his efforts. 'Do I
detect the ever-so-faint whiff of corruption?' she
asks. Jim's smile is strained but, with Karen on
the Wing, he's got to look after number one.

EPISODE 5 SERIES 2

As Sylvia and Di welcome a new group of prisoners, the notoriety of one precedes her. 'Mad' Tessa Spall lives up to her name: convicted of the gruesome murder of her sister, she's famed for having chewed off a prison officer's ear. She is also HIV-positive. Sylvia quickly identifies her in the sweatbox when she hears a woman screaming and kicking, and orders her to be sent to the Block. Unfortunately, she doesn't bother to validate her assumption. In reality, the screaming woman is Barbara Hunt, a new inmate suffering from claustrophobia. Tessa Spall is free to engineer a straight swap; unbeknown to the officers, Tessa is loose on the Wing, under the guise of Barbara.

Karen's new initiative, a group-therapy course, is launched. Dominic tries to persuade Shell to attend: it might be a good way back on Enhanced. She dominates the session, refusing to take it seriously until the therapist probes a little deeper. 'Why do you feel guilty about sex, Michelle?' the therapist asks, stopping Shell in her tracks.

In the Block, Dominic attempts to talk to the woman they believe is Tessa. Barbara, still

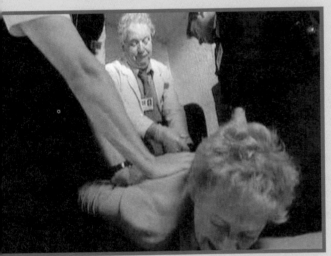

panicking and heavily sedated, cannot explain to him that there has been a mix-up. Tessa's arrival is reported to Karen and her alarm suggests that she has encountered the prisoner before.

The real Tessa, meanwhile, is establishing herself on the Wing and impresses Sylvia with her polite compliance with instructions. Shell senses new prey and tries to intimidate Tessa: 'I'm the governor around here'. Tessa's savage response leaves Shell terrorised. Nikki, reacting to cries for help, looks into the cell. She is stunned to find it is not the new girl but Shell who is in distress. Shell, having met her match, is meekly picking up the remnants of Tessa's dinner off the floor. Tessa is reluctant to blow her cover and plays innocent but Nikki is immediately suspicious.

Visiting day arrives and Yvonne is particularly looking forward to it. She has spent the past week living the lie that Charlie has liver cancer, just for appearances. Jim has promised to show 'compassion' and arrange a private room for her and her husband to discuss things in. At the end of their hour together, they straighten their clothes and share a private laugh at Jim; he seems to think he can call the shots on their little deal. Fenner clearly doesn't know who he's dealing with this time. He has insisted on being paid, off-site, by Charlie himself, who leaves the money in Jim's bag while he plays a round of golf. Unknown to Jim, his photo is taken when he collects the cash.

In the exercise yard, Tessa becomes increasingly agitated when Di cannot confirm when she will get her induction with the Wing Governor. Di promises to arrange it. Satisfied, Tessa looks for trouble elsewhere, in the form of Nikki Wade. She has a go at her, accusing Nikki of interfering in her run-in with Shell. When her insults do not provoke a response, she lashes out and Nikki retaliates. As ever, Jim insists Nikki is to blame and she's demoted to Basic. Dominic, however, isn't convinced that Nikki's actions were unprovoked. When Nikki mentions that 'Barbara' is a 'headcase', he suspects there has been a terrible mistake.

Di gives Tessa some good news: Karen will see her now. On the pretence of fetching her notepad, Tessa collects a hypodermic needle and fills it with her HIV-infected blood. Meanwhile, Dominic raises the alarm – the wrong prisoner is in solitary and Mad Tessa is at large on the Wing. Horrified, he learns that Di has just escorted her to Karen's office.

'Hello, Miss Betts,' Tessa begins, 'Remember me?' Karen looks up from her work to see Tessa holding an infected needle, inches from her face. Karen, petrified, tries to remain calm but Tessa launches into a tirade blaming Karen for spitefully splitting her up from her old cellmate at a previous prison. 'You knew what would happen to me, you knew that my head would go pop, you just didn't give a toss.' Karen's defence – that her cell-mate, Debbie, was frightened of her possessiveness and had asked to be separated – incites only more anger. 'She said it was you I had to blame for everything!' Tessa cries. 'Yes, I know – because that's what I told her to tell you,' Karen replies.

Tessa demands to leave the prison with Karen. As the two women walk towards the gate, Dominic phones ahead to tell the officer there to stall them. Jim goes the back route and begins to unravel the fire hose in the yard. Unable to deter an increasingly agitated Tessa for any longer, Karen is forced to accompany them through to the front gate. Jim calls out to Tessa and, as she turns, he opens fire with the hose, knocking her to the ground. When she is eventually overcome, with the needle out of

reach, she is escorted to the solitary block, leaving a wet and shaken Karen.

On the Wing, Nikki finds herself with a new roommate. Barbara has finally been released from the Block and, owing to her claustrophobia, is to share. Nikki is less than pleased: as a lifer, she should not have to 'two-up', but Hollamby couldn't care less.

EPISODE 6 SERIES 2

Life for Karen Betts has quickly returned to normal following her scare with Mad Tessa Spall, but she blames Sylvia for the mix-up and criticises her 'jobsworth' attitude. Much to the delight of the inmates, Karen finds her own punishment for Sylvia: a fitness-training course. Karen praises Jim Fenner for his quick thinking in saving her but doesn't buy his self-effacing act in turning down the chance of a medal: 'You don't have to overdo it,' she cautions. Nonetheless, she has seen a different side to him.

In the group-therapy session, Shell admits to having nightmares about men. There is one man in particular, 'a bad man', never more than a shadow but someone she knows. As the bell goes to end the session, she is still lost in dark thoughts. That night, the bad man returns in her dreams. She wakes in a cold sweat.

Barbara has other concerns about nightly visits. After hearing that Nikki is a lesbian

she's uncomfortable and is determined not to incite her cellmate's 'unnatural' lust, so goes to bed unwashed and in a full-length dressing gown. In the morning, she approaches Fenner who, ever sympathetic to a grievance about Nikki, takes the opportunity to reproach Nikki in front of Barbara. Nikki is furious and encourages Barbara to move cells if she'd feel safer. As Nikki points out, Barbara's next cellmate could be a junkie – or worse, Shell.

Shell, finally confronting her demons, is slowly losing her mind. Dressed in a micro-skirt and hair bunches at the next therapy session, she announces that she likes getting the attention of men. Meg, the therapist, sees that Shell is on the brink of a breakdown and suggests some time alone at the end of the session. Shell admits to hating men because they all expect sex and take it anyway whether she's offering it or not. 'That's what's always happened,' she says quietly, all bravado evaporated, 'it's been going on all my life, see, ever since I can remember.'

At lock-up, Dominic touches Shell's arm to encourage her into her cell. It is enough: she calls him a sick pervert, accusing him of 'touching her up'. The rest of the women are carried along in the fervour and shout their encouragement. Shell warms to her theme: 'I can't walk down the landing without them all having a grope. I was gang-banged this morning.' Karen attempts to calm the situation. Realising the fragile mental state Shell is in, she strikes a deal offering her job in the kitchen back if she behaves herself. Shell is enthusiastic, adding that she could get a knife and kill Fenner.

By morning, the Wing is in unison with cries of 'rapist' and 'pervert' ringing around the halls. Denny accuses Fenner of voyeurism, while the two Julies tell a confused Dominic that

his peep-show days are over.

Shell, still acting erratically, demands that Barbara smuggle her a black marker from the art class. Shell draws a moustache on herself before demanding that Barbara writes 'Fenner is a rapist' on the wall. After adding a dead body, Shell's work is done. Barbara is horrified but Nikki, walking past, is still reeling from Barbara's betrayal and is unsympathetic. Besides, Nikki has more immediate concerns; she has a visitor. Helen sits across from her, the atmosphere charged as both try to find the words to sum up their feelings at their reunion. When asked about her work situation, Helen claims to have 'one or two irons in the fire,' but is more interested in discussing Nikki. Would she consider appealing against her sentence?

It is not long before the graffiti in the corridor is noticed but Barbara is too scared to grass on Shell and admits to everything, despite Karen's scepticism. Nikki becomes impatient: 'Oh, for God's sake, Dockley did it,' she interrupts. Later, Barbara asks why Nikki intervened to help her: 'I hate Dockley more than I hate you, darling, that's all.' Nevertheless, Barbara is indebted to Nikki and is remorseful about her earlier behaviour.

Sylvia manages to get signed off from her fitness training with claims that her neck is still hurting from her fall. Karen is fast losing patience and, when Fenner shows her a newspaper clipping of Sylvia dancing, she finally has the fuel she needs to haul Sylvia over the coals again. She demands that she start behaving like a senior officer.

Shell reveals to Karen that her father and mother abused her. They brainwashed her into thinking it was all her fault and she has maintained the belief that she must have wanted it. 'It's never because the child wants it,' Karen tells her. Shell's face clouds; if it wasn't her fault then her own children might be at risk – her mother looks after them. Hatred, confusion and fear overwhelm her and she breaks down, crying bitterly on Karen's shoulder.

In the library, Helen sneaks up on Nikki, who is delighted to learn that she has secured a job as a Prison Service Professional with Area Management. They will be seeing a lot more of each other...

Shell is allowed back from the Block, promising that she is feeling much better. However, as Karen and Dominic walk down the hall Denny lets out a scream. Shell is on the landing, dressed in a white sheet, a stocking noose around her neck. 'Come on Mr Fenner, why don't you string me up like Rachel Hicks – it's what you want, innit?' she screams.

EPISODE 7 | SERIES 2

Jim pays Yvonne a visit in her cell. He complains that the money he is receiving for their private visiting room deal is not enough. He needs ample compensation for a worst-case scenario. Yvonne tells Charlie about his demands – Jim needs to realise who he is dealing with. He soon does, when Yvonne smuggles in photographs of him accepting the bribes from Charlie. The tables turned, Yvonne has yet more plans. Fenner is going to help her escape from Larkhall for good.

The prison officers display mixed reactions when learning of Helen's return. Fenner's animosity hasn't waned and he eagerly taunts her about having visited Nikki: 'I have to admit, I didn't realise you were that way inclined, Helen. The signs were there, I suppose,' he smirks. His thinly veiled threats to report his suspicions about their relationship to Stubberfield are dismissed. Helen has already told him of their friendship; she is a professional after all.

The prisoners, in contrast, welcome her back enthusiastically. None more so than Nikki: 'Do you want to come back to my place?' she propositions. Once alone, Nikki expresses doubt about her appeal, not wishing to build her hopes up on a pipe dream, but Helen

refuses to be pessimistic and promises to go through Nikki's files for helpful evidence. She will do everything in her power to get Nikki out of Larkhall so that they can be together.

Zandra is off the smack but her health is rapidly deteriorating. She tries to read a magazine but finds herself unable to focus and flings down her new, useless glasses in frustration. Headaches have been constantly plaguing her and now they're accompanied by violent fits. The prison doctor is not taking her seriously.

Barbara is keeping a diary; once she is released, she intends turning her notes into a book. When Nikki comments that she would rather forget about life inside after she is free, Barbara tells her that she is doing it to stay sane. Gaining trust in her, she tells Nikki about her conviction. Her beloved husband was dying of cancer and, when he begged her to help him die, she believed she was doing the right thing. The courts were unmoved and she was charged with manslaughter. She professes that her loneliness without him provides more punishment than anything prison can offer.

Jim is terrified; finally in a situation he can't wriggle out of, he is set to escort Yvonne out of Larkhall to see her 'ailing' husband. She will then set up an escape. Jim is fretting and looking for an ally. When Karen walks into the office, he admits to still resenting her

for believing Shell's story over his own in the assault allegation. 'I felt I had good reason,' Karen says evenly. Suddenly his regrets overwhelm him and Jim comes close to confessing all, but, interrupted by Sylvia's bustling entrance, he must make do with, 'I'm sorry'.

Yvonne announces that the escape plan is to happen that day, which sends shock waves to Jim, who is completely out of his depth. He is not the only unhappy one; in the library, Helen tells Nikki that her files have only produced bad news. The judge at her trial ordered she serve ten years before parole would even be considered. In addition, because she killed a police officer, there is a possibility that she may never be released. Helen, barely able to ask, needs Nikki to reassure her that she isn't the cold-blooded killer described in the files. Nikki can easily give her that comfort. Needing some time alone, they head to the art room, but Helen breaks Nikki's impassioned kiss. 'There's no signposts anymore,' she tells Nikki, wracked with confusion. She tries to explain that Nikki has turned her life upside down – that she has never loved a woman before and that she is coming to terms with the changes in her life. Nikki is reassuring: 'You're not normal, you're not abnormal – you do what you want, what you feel'. However, Nikki also needs confirmation from Helen that she is committed to their relationship. Helen reassures her and says that, what's more, she will not rest until Nikki is free.

Visiting time brings a surprise for Yvonne. Her daughter, Lauren, is extremely agitated but her tears are not the ones she rehearsed for her father's fictitious illness. Charlie has been arrested and this time the charges will stick. Jim sees the scene and assumes the act is going to plan, but Yvonne is doing some fast thinking. The compassionate license goes ahead but Yvonne complains of a stomach upset. The car is pulled over outside a pub and Sylvia and Yvonne head into the ladies, where Yvonne locks herself in the cubicle and makes a bid for freedom out of the window. Jim, waiting outside, glances at a newspaper to see the news of Charlie Atkins' arrest on the front page. He realises Yvonne is trying to escape and that, with Charlie inside, he can now stop her. Dragging her back through the tiny window, Jim is back on top again.

Zandra returns to the Wing after finally securing tests for her persistent headaches from an outside hospital. As she is welcomed back, she confirms she is feeling much better after they dosed her with painkillers. She is relieved that, with proper medical care, she can now look forward to getting better. Karen, however, has received a phone call from the hospital: she knows different.

EPISODE 8 SERIES 2

As Yvonne ruefully reads the newspaper report about Charlie's incarceration, she is inspired with an idea to keep the money coming in. The adverts for telephone sex lines are plentiful but she can add a new spin. She approaches the two Julies and Denny with a proposition: they will operate their own scam inside Larkhall. Mobile phones are swiftly smuggled on to the Wing and, ever helpful, Barbara establishes a website advertising their new service. The Julies have decided their roles: 'Whiplash Wanda' and 'Sexy Sonia'. Deciding that Denny's 'Gail' will not pull in the punters, they suggest instead that she is 'Vicky, the Virgin Bride', on the basis that she will not need any expertise. Yvonne sees herself with more authority, announcing that she will play Bodybag. 'Babes Behind Bars' is in business.

Zandra's condition is a source of concern to all the prisoners. In the garden, Barbara

finds Nikki pulling up some cannabis plants. Now that she is planning an appeal, Nikki needs to be squeaky clean. Barbara is reluctant to see an effective herbal remedy go to waste, having previously grown it herself to relieve her late husband's suffering. She takes charge of the plant and later passes it on to Crystal for Zandra. To Crystal, drugs are drugs, and she immediately disposes of the cannabis in the kitchen bins. Dominic has also been worried about Zandra since Karen confided to him that the prognosis did not look good. A further scan is needed to assess her operability, and Dominic volunteers to be Zandra's escort.

Karen has suggested calling a private meeting to allow Shell to confront her mother and lay to rest the ghosts from her past. Shell cannot find peace until she has assured herself that her own children are safe in their grandmother's care. She is terrified of confronting her mother but Karen is supportive.

Rita Dockley, Shell's mother, immediately blames the officers for her daughter's pallid and vacant demeanour. Shell ventures to ask how her children are, but Rita brushes this aside, telling her she needs to worry about herself: 'You got to get your fight back, girl. Get the old swagger back.' As she continues to talk, Shell stops listening, hearing instead the ghostly voices from her childhood as she pleaded for her parents to stop the abuse. Eventually, Rita grows impatient with Shell's silence and spits: 'You've turned my daughter into a zombie, ain't ya?' Shell finally breaks: 'All my life, always fobbing off the blame, weren't you? Well I can see you now, Mum, what you done to me...what you let Dad do to me!' Rita wildly refutes the allegations but Shell is steeled. She will ask social services to put her children into care. Back in her cell, she quietly says goodbye to them, kissing a photo of her daughters before tearing it up.

Zandra receives her test results, and the worst is confirmed by an insensitive Dr Nicholson. She has a malignant brain tumour, with no possibility of a cure and no recommended course of action other than painkillers. She will die in months rather than years. Surrounded by her friends later, she is in shock. While the other prisoners curse Dr 'No-No' Nicholson's inaction and lack of care, Karen has a meeting with him and Dominic. Nicholson is scornful of Karen's suggestion of alternative therapy, claiming that Zandra has already battered her system with drugs to such an extent that there is little point. Dominic flies into a temper, disgusted at their treatment of a dying teenager. Karen is more level-headed and has already ordered an enquiry into prison health care. She also arranges for Zandra's temporary freedom, which can be extended by a doctor indefinitely for health reasons. Dominic tells

Zandra the good news but she has nowhere to go. Her only option is Crystal, who is due for release, but she can't go to someone's home just to die. Crystal asks Josh if Zandra can stay with them but Josh refuses: this is their first chance to be together.

The 'Babes Behind Bars' team have been instructed by Yvonne to hide their phones in their bras. Denny is taken by surprise when her cleavage vibrates as she receives the first call. Things do not go to plan: 'Lick *what* off?' she snaps, 'You're one seriously sick geezer!' She cuts the caller off. The Julies are in despair: 'You're on a bleeding telephone sex line!' they hiss. But when the punter calls again, Denny realises she may have a talent for sex lines after all: 'You're saying you want a bad-mouthed bitch? I ain't even started on you yet.'

Meanwhile, Crystal is bitterly regretting her decision to bin the cannabis, especially when Nikki points out that Zandra may be prescribed heroin on the outside. Nikki reveals that most inmates use Josh for contraband and, although Crystal is furious with him, she enlists his services. He will bring in proper painkillers for Zandra. Crystal then makes an even greater sacrifice: she retrieves the cannabis from the bins and posts an anonymous note to the prison officers, informing on herself. A quick search later and she is given additional days to her sentence, just when she is about to be released. Zandra will not be alone. As Crystal winks at her before being escorted to the Block, Zandra cannot thank her closest friend enough. Less pleased by the development is Josh, waiting to no avail for Crystal outside the prison on the day of her release – engagement ring in hand.

EPISODE 9 SERIES 2

News of Zandra's diagnosis has spread across the Wing and, in addition to her own pain and fear of death, she suffers the stares and awkwardness of those who are unsure of how to react. Zandra has come to depend heavily on Dominic and a deep affection grows between them. Nonetheless, she is ecstatic when Crystal returns from the Block: 'You're the best mate ever,' she whispers. Her gratitude for Crystal's sacrifice is in stark contrast to Josh's feelings. He fumes to Crystal that he doesn't want to marry a saint and hands her the engagement ring, claiming he no longer wants it. She has lost her chance of a life with him.

Shell, having faced the ghosts of her past, returns to being her old self. She looks for someone to bully and selects Barbara. Shell steals Barbara's diary from her cell, and sits down for a good read. Barbara catches her and is outraged but Shell refuses to give it back

until she is good and finished. Barbara looks to Nikki for help but Nikki tells her that, while she could easily confront Dockley on her behalf, it would ultimately solve nothing: 'You can't keep running away or she'll make your life hell,' she insists.

After lights out, Zandra feels alone and scared, and asks to join Crystal in her bunk. As Crystal holds her, she admits to being scared of dying. 'It's not dying,' Crystal whispers, 'It's like walking out of prison into the fresh air and the sunshine, leaving all the bad things behind.' In an attempt to make peace, Zandra begins to pray: 'Now I lay me down to sleep...'

Dominic feels useless over Zandra's plight. Zandra, however, insists to him: 'You help me get through,' and confesses that she daydreams about what could have been. Dominic gently lifts her face to his and they share a delicate kiss. 'I shouldn't have done that, I'm sorry,' Dominic blurts out, springing away. Zandra just smiles: 'Don't be. At least one of my dreams came true.'

Wanting to bring some joy to Zandra's life, the Julies arrange a small party in the dorm, with miniatures provided by Yvonne. Dominic knows full well what they are up to but allows them one hour for Zandra's sake. Shell sees an opportunity to taunt Barbara by reciting her diary in front of the others. She selects quotes criticising the assembled prisoners hoping that they will be suitably offended and turn on Barbara. Instead, the reception is unanimously frosty towards Shell for invading Barbara's privacy. As Barbara apologises for the things she wrote in her diary, she admits she was ignorant but has since changed her opinions of all of them apart from Shell. Zandra takes the lead and asks Shell to leave. Shell is all bravado until she is on her own and realises she truly is alone.

The party continues when Julie S.'s mobile phone vibrates. She is surprised at the punter's request: 'He wants me to baa!' she whispers, 'Like a sheep!' The women laugh uncontrollably, all imitating farmyard animals. Crystal tries not to be too amused. She looks over to Zandra who is laughing along until she suddenly stops, her cigarette falling from her fingers. Even before Zandra slumps to the floor, Crystal knows this is it. After a short but violent fit, Zandra Plackett lies still.

The memorial service is an emotional time for staff and inmates alike. Dominic has managed to arrange for baby Robbie to attend and Crystal reads out a letter Zandra left her to read after her death. Zandra has thanked all of her friends for their support – particularly Crystal – and the congregation is deeply moved. Zandra's letter finishes with a request: 'I want you to sing 'Kumbaya' when you've finished this, not because I like it but because it used to drive old Bodybag mad when we sang it all the time.'

That evening Crystal feigns illness. When Dr Nicholson comes to visit her, she tells him exactly what she thinks – that he is responsible for Zandra's death: 'You didn't give a toss, did you and you don't now, neither,' she shouts. 'The Lord knows, though, doesn't he?' she says menacingly, 'He'll make sure you burn in hell.' Spitting in his face, she adds: 'That's for Zandra.' Back on the Block, Crystal sits on the bed, running her fingers over Josh's

engagement ring. She has lost the two people she cares about; she finally allows herself to cry.

Barbara decides to confront Shell once Nikki assures her she will intervene if necessary. She strides with affected confidence into Shell's room and demands the return of her book. After appearing non-committal, Shell suddenly pins Barbara to the bed. Barbara cries out but Nikki reluctantly walks away: Barbara must face Shell alone. Shell taunts Barbara about her husband: 'I bet he wasn't dying of cancer at all, was he? I bet you just got sick of him.' Barbara is consumed with rage and, wrestling herself free, flings Shell against the wall: 'Don't you dare even say his name, do you hear, not ever?' she shouts as Shell crouches, whimpering in pain.

As Dominic leaves for home, he glances up at the window where Zandra had so often been looking out for him. It is empty and he says his own, silent goodbye.

EPISODE 10   SERIES 2

Julie J. has become broody, having looked after little Robbie at Zandra's memorial service and contemplated her own estranged children. Julie S. has a simple answer: have another child. Julie J. considers this new idea and decides it might work; she needs to get pregnant, however, and in a women's prison the opportunities are limited.

Julie J. does not let the short supply of men dampen her enthusiasm. She approaches Dominic in the gardens but, once he gets wind of her plan, he flees. The next stop is the prison chaplain, but his opening gambit of: 'Whatever your problem, I'm your man,' proves ultimately misleading. The only other option is the ever-ready Fenner but Julie decides she's not that desperate. Just when the Julies are about to give up, a punter phones looking for a 'Babe behind Bars' – it is John, one of the regulars. He seems nice enough and Julie J. has an idea.

On the Wing, Shell nurses a sprained arm, having come off distinctly worse in her altercation with Barbara. Karen's attempts to find the guilty party fail. Shell insists that her injury was the result of a fall, and no one else is going to grass on Barbara. No one, that is, except Barbara herself: guilt-ridden, she confesses. Karen asks Shell for confirmation but Shell is horrified, as her reputation will be in tatters if the women believe middle-aged Barbara got the better of her: 'The old cow's barmy, I just fell over – no one's laid a finger on me!' Karen therefore has no choice but to let the matter drop.

In reception, Dominic takes an instant dislike to a new arrival. Renee Williams is bolshy, fearless and an utterly dislikable bigot. She is also smuggling a razor blade in her mouth. Fortunately for those on the Wing, she spends the weekend in the reception dorm: 'Smells like a jungle in here,' she carps. Renee, most definitely, is trouble.

Julie J. is on the phone to John again. Since the resident Larkhall men are unwilling to assist her, he appears to be her best option and she has sent him a visiting order. Julie S. is sceptical of the plan: 'How's he going to get you up the stick in the middle of the bleeding visiting room?' Julie J. is determined, however, and miracles can be worked with an empty yoghurt pot and syringe.

In the four-bed dorm, Denny is finding herself increasingly attracted to the latest occupant, Shaz Wiley. Shaz is one of the youngest inmates on the Wing but impresses them all by revealing she's inside for triple murder. Shaz sets about giving Denny the benefit of the prison training she had while on remand: she and Denny are going to have some fun. Shaz stuffs their cell lock with toilet paper to prevent the door securing. After lock-up, they sneak out to cause mayhem: dropping washing powder tablets into toilet cisterns, filling condoms with water and, to top it all off, rigging up an effigy of Bodybag, with the clever use of a mop, bucket and bin liner. The next day, chaos reigns and laughter flows, as do the toilets. Bodybag, predictably, is not amused. Neither is Karen, who can only

speculate that Larkhall has a phantom, as no one seems to know how the sabotage occurred.

Renee Williams makes her presence felt as soon as she arrives on the Wing. Yvonne looks distinctly uneasy, and reveals to Barbara that she is doing time for trying to dispatch Renee's husband by taking a contract out on him. Renee immediately establishes that she is boss of her four-bed dorm. 'This is *Renee's* room, ok?' When Denny, trying to impress Shaz, retaliates, Renee produces the razor blade and threatens it an inch away from Denny's face.

John's appearance in the flesh is not promising, bearing little similarity to a photo he sent. But this could be Julie J.'s one chance and, with yoghurt pot at the ready, she puts her plan into action. However, she is not as deft as the job requires and, after an ungainly fumble under the visiting room table, the pot clatters to the floor. John, realising Julie's objective, leaps to his feet. 'This is a scam,' he shouts, silencing the room. 'Nine months down the line, you're going to hit me with a paternity suit.'

The two Julies are hauled before Karen. John has spilled the beans about the 'Babes Behind Bars' scam. Karen refuses to believe the Julies could have run the operation themselves and orders a search of the entire Wing for more mobile phones. Yvonne reacts quickly, ordering Denny to stash them in the loos. They escape discovery but the Babes have had their day.

As Yvonne fumes at how stupid the two Julies have been, Renee sidles up to her. She taunts Yvonne about her husband's imprisonment: 'At least you know Charlie ain't poking any other women,' she sneers. The other women are amazed that Yvonne does not react. Yvonne, aware of the razor blade and of Renee's disposition, doesn't want to provoke her. Her composure slips, however, when Renee talks about a small scar Charlie has on the most intimate part of his body. There is only one way she can know about this and it's obvious that Charlie has been messing around with his enemy's wife. Yvonne is devastated and, escaping to her cell, dissolves into tears.

EPISODE 11 SERIES 2

Renee Williams' reign of terror continues as Crystal arrives back from her punishment on the Block. Even Crystal, armed with the Lord on her side, can't help but be intimidated. Renee has singled her out for special attention: she doesn't like the colour of her skin. But Renee has bigger fish to fry and, emerging from a toilet cubicle, she attacks Yvonne with her razor blade. Nikki's quick thinking saves Yvonne from serious injury but Yvonne knows it will only be a matter of time before Renee tries again. She has to find a way of despatching her for good.

Still buzzing from their night of mayhem, Denny and Shaz are eager to break out after lock-up again. Luring Hollamby into their cell, they bolt past her and lock her in, forcing her to surrender her keys. With Bodybag confined, they are free to embark on an excursion to the servery, where Denny collects treats while Shaz selects some mouldy bread from the bins, to add to Renee's orange juice. Renee is violently sick. Payback.

Helen is getting to grips with her new role as Life Sentence Liaison Governor (L.S.L.G.). At her new lifers' group, she shares illicit glances with Nikki but manages to retain her composure. At the end of the session, the others leave Helen and Nikki alone but Dominic interrupts their clandestine moment. With no hope of privacy in Larkhall, Nikki writes a letter to Helen, declaring her love.

Yvonne notices Renee's obsessive questioning of Shell on the content of the prison food, and deduces that Renee has a nut allergy. She researches the condition in the library and discovers to her delight that the condition is deadly. She hatches a plan. As the Wing watches on – all with their personal grudges – Renee liberally sprinkles pepper onto her food. Within seconds, Renee's self-satisfied face contorts in terror. She gasps for air and falls to the ground, choking, before she stops breathing. Yvonne has spiked the pepper pot with crushed nuts. A police investigation ensues but, unaware as yet of the exact cause of death, they can only deduce that she's been poisoned by an inmate. As Renee had so many enemies, everyone appears to be a suspect.

Hollamby knows that Shaz and Denny had access to the servery and ergo the rat poison on the floor during their night-time walkabout. She begins to panic as, out of shame at her own stupidity, she omitted to report Shaz and Denny's brief escape. She confesses her error to Jim in the officers' club, where Jim is spending an increasing amount of time. He is unsympathetic: 'Admit it, Sylvia, you've been a stupid bitch'. He advises her to tell Karen immediately before anyone else does. Karen is livid: 'You neglected your duties with disastrous, possibly tragic consequences! You're lucky you're not being sacked!' Karen asks

for Sylvia's pips and demotes her to a basic grade officer.

Shaz's record as a poisoner makes her the police's number-one suspect. When they learn from a mortified Karen that Shaz had access to the servery, the police accuse her of spiking Renee's drink with the rat poison. Having tampered with Renee's orange juice the night before her death, Shaz believes she may well have killed her. Shaz reasons that, as she has three life sentences already, she won't notice another, and promptly confesses to the crime. Yvonne, horrified that Shaz is taking the rap, tells Denny that Shaz could get herself shipped out to a 'loony bin'.

Meanwhile, Nikki has an encouraging meeting with her new lawyer, who is a friend of Helen's. She is optimistic about Nikki's chances of appeal, on the grounds that the policeman Nikki killed had a violent history. However, the easy familiarity between the lawyer and Helen perturbs Nikki. Helen reiterates to her that she has never had a relationship with a woman before and implores Nikki not to be jealous. Nikki, though, can only imagine Helen's life away from work and is irrationally consumed by the green-eyed monster. Helen insists that she shares the emotions Nikki describes in her letter, however Nikki is beyond convincing. Her suspicions only increase when she overhears Helen arrange a dinner with Dominic.

With Yvonne's warning about Shaz ringing in her ears, Denny goes to the police and confesses to the murder herself. They give her short shrift, content that they have found their killer. However, their satisfaction is short-lived when a phone call confirms that Renee died of anaphylactic shock, induced by a nut allergy. Under such circumstances, no one can be blamed for her murder. Karen is relieved as she announces the news to an equally pleased G-Wing. However, Shaz and Denny's rejoicing is short-lived, as Karen orders a belated spell down on the Block as punishment for their break-out.

As G-Wing celebrates, Karen has a loose end to tie up: why was Jim not on the Wing when Renee collapsed and died? She is disturbed by his recent erratic behaviour and pays him a visit after work. She finds his living room in disarray and discovers that his wife has left him. 'I'm a failure,' he says, breaking down. 'I've lost everything. She's taken the kids and I don't know where they are.' Karen can only cradle Jim as he weeps on to her shoulder.

EPISODE 12 SERIES 2

Nikki is indifferent to Helen's continued interest in her appeal. Her attention is focused instead on Helen's recent 'date' with Dominic. Reassurances from Helen that it was all in the cause of work do not suffice and Nikki is stubborn. In an angry encounter in the prison gardens, Helen loses her patience: 'Sod you, Nikki'.

Karen allows Denny and Shaz out of the Block. Shaz is unrepentant about their pranks and Renee's death: 'There's you lot saying we done murder on her and all it took were a nut'. Karen isn't impressed and points out that Shaz's lasting inheritance from Renee will be to assume her 'bog brush duty'.

Helen is growingly concerned about Shaz's blasé attitude to prison and the horrendous crime that put her there. Shaz is perfectly content, all things considered, and maintains

that her crime was an accident. She spiked oysters at the fish counter she worked at merely to get back at her bossy manager. She didn't mean to kill anyone, so she doesn't have to feel guilty. Besides, she adds, two of her victims were old and would have died soon anyway. Helen is appalled and realises that drastic action is required. She informs Shaz that she will never get parole with her present attitude. The only way she can face up to the magnitude of her crime is by meeting one of her victims' relatives.

Nikki attempts to apologise to Helen for her jealousy, but she can't stop her insecurities from surfacing again. She believes Helen will leave her for a man – the first in line being the doting Dominic. Helen insists that it's irrelevant if Dominic fancies her or not; Nikki should stop assuming that Helen will be fickle in her feelings.

Fenner is back at work, looking the worse for wear following his separation from his wife. His colleagues begin to notice that his behaviour is odd, and suspect he is drinking on duty. When trouble erupts in the servery, Di quickly loses control of the situation. Jim won't help and publicly interprets Di's pleas for assistance as evidence that she can't do her job. A furious Di accuses him of undermining her authority in front of the women. The inmates love the spectacle. Nikki takes advantage of the mayhem and decides to phone Helen in order to resolve their earlier quarrels.

Dominic turns up at Helen's flat on the pretext of work, with a bottle of drink under his arm. He cautiously approaches the subject of relationships and hints at his attraction to her. Helen is amiable but tries to remain detached. The phone rings and Dominic picks it up to hand to Helen. When he drops the receiver, Nikki, on the other end of the line, hears his

fumbled apology. She hangs up, consumed by a fresh wave of jealousy and mistrust. Helen realises what has happened and tries to affect apathy but Dominic misreads her body language and attempts to kiss her. Helen stops him and realises she must come clean: she is in love with someone else – another woman. Needing to finally say the words aloud, she confesses to Dominic that it is Nikki Wade. He promises to retain her counsel but is stunned and disappointed.

Karen confronts Jim on his recent conduct and reluctantly threatens to suspend him. Her leniency takes him by surprise and he apologises, promising to also make amends with Di. Karen's eyes show her appreciation.

Helen finds Nikki in the garden and tries to explain to her why Dominic was in her flat. Nikki, however, has already formed her own conclusions. Her aggression forces Helen to pull rank. Nikki responds: 'Don't worry – I won't forget to call you "Miss"'. This is the last straw for Helen: 'I am so sick of you!' she replies and walks away. Nikki returns to her gardening but, preoccupied by her anger, accidentally stabs her fork into her hand.

Helen is in turmoil and is wracked by the strain of Nikki's paranoia. Dominic speaks to Nikki, telling her he knows it is she whom Helen loves. Nikki belatedly tries to apologise to Helen, but is too late and she is told to: 'Go and fall for someone else.'

A reluctant Shaz finally has to face a meeting with the widow of one of her victims. Mrs Foster is a wise old bird and Shaz learns a few home truths. As Shaz ventures an unconvincing apology, Mrs Foster challenges her: 'You're kidding yourself, dear, you've only got as far as being sorry for yourself'. She describes the loss she experienced because of Shaz's actions: 'Don't ever think that old age makes you more ready to die. When your time is running out, it just makes it all the more precious.'

Shaz finally realises the pain and tragedy her crime has caused: 'You hate me, don't you?' she sobs. Mrs Foster is generous and philosophical: 'No, I hate what you did but I don't hate you.' As Denny later comforts her, Shaz admits she cannot cope with her guilt and wants to die. Denny reassures her that she loves her and that dying would be the coward's way out. She must just find a way of making up for her crime.

Jim tells Karen that Marilyn has started divorce proceedings. He is glad it is all over. Karen pours him a drink and they toast freedom but, setting their glasses down, they find comfort in each other instead. Compelled towards each other, they kiss.

EPISODE 13 SERIES 2

On the Wing, Nikki is fretting over the finality of Helen's rejection. She convinces herself she could patch things up if they could just get some time together out of Larkhall. She resolves to escape for just one night to spend it with Helen. Nikki recalls that the prison nurse who tended her wounded hand was desperate to go to Australia, and she hatches a plan. She asks her ex-girlfriend, Trish, for some cash. Exactly the amount the nurse said she needed for her flight.

The foundations laid, Nikki reopens her wound and asks to see the nurse again. She passes Helen on the way, who, seeing her bandaged hand and pained expression, is concerned despite her bitterness. The nurse balks at Nikki's proposition but the cash is too tempting and she eventually agrees. In exchange for the money, she will help Nikki engineer her escape, using the cover of Bodybag's 30th wedding anniversary party, to be held at the prison officers' club.

Yvonne eagerly awaits an inter-prison visit from Charlie but Bodybag bluntly informs her it is cancelled: 'He said he doesn't want to see you again – and that's from the horse's mouth.' Yvonne is broken-hearted. Jim Fenner is anything but sympathetic and revels in spelling out what she has been denying to herself: that her beloved Charlie set her up to continue his affair with Renee.

Crystal is finally due to leave Larkhall. But before she goes, she helps herself to Sylvia's presentation clock; her kleptomania is not quite in check. Crystal's cautious hopes of Josh being at the gates are dashed and she spends her first evening of freedom alone. Her hostel room is lonelier than her cell, so she goes to a café where she picks at a stodgy celebration dinner for one.

Those chosen to waitress at Sylvia's party plan their own celebration – by emptying the alcohol slops into makeshift pouches to take back to their cells. There is a frisson between Karen and Fenner that doesn't escape the eagle eyes of Yvonne, who points it out to Shell. 'Miss Betts wouldn't touch Fenner,' Shell scoffs. Yvonne is not so sure: 'I'd say she was shagging him.' Shell is disgusted. Karen has been good to her and she resolves to repay the favour by warning the Wing Governor off: 'He did hit me, Miss, you know he did.' Meanwhile, Dominic has arrived to a gushing reception from Di, who has bought a dress especially for the occasion. Limpeting herself to him, she whisks him off for a dance, only to snap a shoulder strap in her vigour.

On the Wing, Nikki's prediction is right: the night officer is more than happy to surrender his keys to the nurse so he can join the party. As Nikki creates a dummy in her bed and dons a blonde wig, the nurse escorts her out. Narrowly escaping Di, Nikki easily bluffs her way past the gate lodge. She is free.

Back at the party, Yvonne suggests to the girls that they slip an 'E' into Sylvia's drink. It

quickly takes effect and her frenetic dancing starts to exhaust her husband Bobby. Flinging herself at Dominic instead, she gives Bobby the two-fingered salute and he leaves the club without her.

Helen answers her door and is aghast to find Nikki standing there. Helen is furious, remonstrating at Nikki's impetuousness. Nikki, however, did not come to fight: 'Tell me you love me,' she beseeches. Helen's defences dissolve and she relaxes into Nikki's embrace. Their kiss increases in urgency as long-repressed passions are released and Helen finally succumbs to her desires.

As the party draws to a close, a dishevelled Sylvia refuses Karen's offer of a taxi. Instead, she careers into the table full of slops intended for the inmates' pouches, much to their exasperation. Di engineers a shared cab ride with Dominic and invites him in for a coffee. Dominic agrees warily but leaves when Di's bed-ridden mother calls for her. A distressed Di goes to her bedroom and gazes at her shrine to Dominic, comprising items she has stolen from him as keepsakes.

In Helen's arms, Nikki is optimistic about the future, until she sees a letter on Helen's bedside table. 'I'm sorry, sweetheart, it's bad news,' Helen confesses her appeal has been turned down but insists it's not the end of the road. Nikki is devastated. She decides their only hope of a life together is for her to not return to Larkhall. Helen is adamant: a life on the run is no life at all. But Nikki will not be dissuaded and asks Helen to phone for a taxi. Nikki goes to get dressed and Helen picks up the phone – and dials 999.

Crystal, feeling desperately alone, returns to her hostel to discover she has been locked out. Hearing her name called, she turns to see Josh standing behind her. She tells him she is still wearing his engagement ring – is it what he wants to hear? He invites her back to stay with him. Crystal smiles: 'Got no choice, innit?'

Karen, in mind of Shell's warning, rejects Jim's advances. Frustrated, he goes to lock Shell in for the night. She pleads with him to allow her one little kiss and apologises for her betrayal. 'You're learning, love,' he accepts. They sink onto the bed and, while sighing under Jim's caresses, Shell reaches for the broken bottle she has smuggled from the party. Revenge will be sweet, if a little sharp.

You Know You're a *Bad Girls* Fan When...

1. You paint your skirting boards green
2. You replace your best china tea service with blue plastic mugs
3. You get someone to lock you in your room at night, and then check on your progress through a hatch
4. You have your shopping delivered by swinger
5. You say 'twatting' at the beginning of each sentence and 'innit' at the end
6. You buy a potting shed, despite having no garden
7. You dye all your sheets dirty brown
8. You move your loo into the bedroom and line the seat with sanitary towels
9. You wear an orange netball bib whenever visitors come round
10. You try to pay for everything with phone cards
11. You ensure that your bra strap is visible at all times
12. You have 'Kumbaya' as your mobile phone ring-tone, or you just have it on vibrate
13. You feel superior if you have a flat on the third floor
14. You ignore the wine your guest brings and serve straight vodka
15. You show your rebellious nature by forming a choir
16. You baah when you answer your phone
17. You fill your pepper pot with crushed nuts
18. You crutch your prescription coming back from the chemist
19. You start an O.U. degree and then forget all about it

20. You get your postman to deliver your packages by throwing them over the garden wall whilst you create a diversion

21. You keep your possessions in a see-through plastic bag

22. You wince when you see a nail and an apple

23. You tell your dying mother 'Shit happens'

24. You get out of sticky situations by tap-dancing to hymns

25. You go to night classes in Glaswegian

26. You keep a broken bottle under the bed (just for emergencies!)

27. You don't serve jellies at children's parties any more

28. You never buy family tubs of marge

29. You order your ankle bracelets from the Home Office

30. You wear your house keys on a long chain

31. You flush dead pets down the loo

32. Your latest boyfriend's name is scrawled on your bedroom mirror

33. You finish your best friend's sentences

34. You'd rather starve than order a home-delivery pizza

35. You go to your solicitor when you want a shag

36. Your kitchen is 'the servery', your local shop 'the canteen' and weekly wages your 'private spends'

37. You stick pictures on the wall with toothpaste

YOU KNOW YOU'RE A REAL BAD GIRLS FAN WHEN YOU UNDERSTAND ALL OF THE ABOVE

(In homage to the original thread on the www.badgirls.co.uk website)

EPISODE 1 SERIES 3

Jim Fenner has played with fire once too many times and Shell now takes her revenge, sticking a broken bottle into his stomach and giving it an agonising twist for good measure. Karen is alerted to his cries but, before she can rescue Fenner, Shell shoves him off her bed and uses it to barricade her cell door. Karen quickly puts an emergency plan into operation, which involves calling the officers from their homes. Sylvia, still in her ballgown and woozy from her gin and Ecstasy cocktail, wobbles into Larkhall.

Meanwhile, back at Helen's house, Nikki is full of love for Helen and is getting set for her flight to freedom across the Atlantic, where she wants Helen to join her. After an agonising internal struggle, Helen decides not to speak to the police. Instead she offers to drive Nikki to her ex-girlfriend, Trish's, place where Nikki plans to pick up her passport. Pretty soon, they're on the road, but Helen isn't going anywhere near Trish's house. She's

heading back to Larkhall and, what's more, Nikki's going with her. Nikki is horrified by Helen's betrayal and tries to steer the car where she wants it to go; the car lurches to left and right. Police in a nearby panda are alerted and it looks like Nikki's cover is going to be blown. However, a friendly, butch officer thinks it's a lovers' tiff and lets them go. Nikki gives up her useless fight: she's going back to Larkhall.

As they approach the prison, Helen's mobile phone rings. She's informed of the emergency on G-Wing and asked to come in. Helen seizes the opportunity in the melee to sneak Nikki back into the prison. Nikki rejoins a very shocked Barbara in her cell and proceeds to sound off about her precious missed opportunity and Helen Bloody Stewart.

Back in Shell's barricaded cell, Jim is bleeding profusely. At first he tries to scare Shell, telling her that she'll never get away with it and she'll rot forever in prison. When she threatens to stick the bottle in his 'pudding', he backs off and begins to plead with her; he's going to die if she doesn't get him medical help. Shell's also oblivious to his pleas – Jim's had it coming and he deserves all he gets. Helen joins Karen on G3. There's an edgy moment as the two women argue about tactics. Karen wants to send the big boys in. Helen urges for a more cautious approach and, since Shell's a lifer, she's Helen's responsibility. Karen stands down, but only for so long...

Meanwhile, the riot team is togging up. Sylvia's very disgruntled at being chosen for the task. She tries to do a deal with Di, asking if she can't stand in for her. But Di has already

been given orders of her own. Sylvia is nervous but has to go through with this. As Jim's life ebbs away, Helen begins her negotiations with Shell. Shell is now beginning to enjoy her fifteen minutes of fame, as her name gets chanted around the prison.

Helen's gambit is to try to buy Shell off with goodies from the prison canteen. Shell orders up a long list and is amazed when it arrives. Helen tells her to open the door so that they can give the things to her. Shell scoffs at this: her name's Shell, 'not Spazza'. Helen is then forced to agree to send the treats up in a swinger – as long as Shell lowers the bottle down. Shell hesitates before agreeing to this condition.

Di, meanwhile, is directed to catch the swinger once it is lowered with the bottle, and to hang on to it. Karen's plan is that the riot officers will ram the door before Shell realises what has happened. Di is in position and on her walkie-talkie as the bottle inches its way down the walls of Larkhall. She radios to her fellow officers, 'Got it!' but, alas, she's speaking prematurely. As Sylvia and her colleagues ram Shell's door, Shell realises that she's been conned. As quickly as she can, she pulls the bottle back into her cell, determined to use it on the now unconscious Jim. However, just before she can retrieve the bottle, the cell door gives way and she's grabbed kicking and screaming from her cell as the prisoners shout abuse at the officers. Jim is rushed to the prison hospital.

Helen tells Nikki that they must suspend their relationship, or the implications for both of them may be devastating. When Nikki rejects her caution as cowardice, Helen has no choice but to let her believe that.

Elsewhere, Karen has the hard task of alerting Marilyn Fenner to what has happened. Marilyn immediately twigs that Dockley has something to do with it. She nevertheless hurries to the hospital to see her estranged husband.

Dr 'No-No' Nicholson looks very uneasy as he applies the electric paddles of the defibrillator machine to Jim's heart area. He urges everyone to stand back. Jim's body lurches violently but there's not a hint of any activity on the heart monitor. The signs don't look good at all.

EPISODE 2 SERIES 3

Jim Fenner's heart is still failing to respond to the defibrillator. Marilyn, who is now by his side, is in despair. Karen is touched and feels guilty, noticing Marilyn's obvious love for him. Dr Nicholson wants to give up, but Karen urges him to try again, with greater power; after an agonising few seconds, the heart monitor springs into life.

Meanwhile, Shell's fate awaits her as she is manhandled along the corridors of the punishment block. Sylvia is furious with her and warns that if Fenner doesn't pull through, her life is going to be made miserable. Shell is all fiery defiance, so Sylvia slaps her hard across the face and advises her colleagues to do the same if she plays up. Shell is then dumped in a cell, screaming blue murder.

A new morning dawns at Larkhall and the women are full of gossip about Shell's assault

on Jim. Shell is not the most popular prisoner on G-Wing, but when it's the screws versus the prisoners, it's the prisoners every time. Unusually, Simon Stubberfield takes the meeting on the Wing. He gives the officers an update on Jim's condition and lets them know that flowers have been sent. Sylvia is on the warpath; she wants to know what is going to happen to Dockley. Simon assures his colleagues that he's looking for a place elsewhere, but then Helen steps in; she is sorry, but any decision about Dockley will be hers. Sylvia is horrified – Helen has always had it in for Jim. She is even more horrified when she hears who will be conducting the enquiry into the incident: Helen.

As Sylvia and Di walk around the Wing, they feel the hostility of the women towards them. Yvonne has a laugh at Jim's expense: 'Mr Fenner not at work today?' It just confirms Sylvia's worst fears: no one cares about them, they've only got each other. And now, with Helen in charge of the enquiry, the whole thing is going to be a whitewash. Sylvia spots Dr Nicholson and an idea forms.

A few days on the block have stripped Shell of her defiance, but she still manages to lie to Helen about Jim's 'rape'. Helen would love to confirm her story, but she can see that Shell is talking 'bullshit'. It looks like her enquiry is going nowhere. Sylvia pitches up at Shell's cell and informs her that: 'The powers that be have decided you're to have a change of scenery.' Shell is puzzled, but not for long. She is led, terrified, into the dreaded psychiatric unit, known as the 'Muppet Wing' to staff and inmates alike. She is thrown into her cell by Betty, the female equivalent of Boris Karloff. Just as Shell thinks things couldn't get worse, her door opens and in comes a blast from the past: Mad Tessa Spall.

Meanwhile, Karen visits Jim in hospital and asks him straight out: what was he doing that night in Shell's cell? He answers without a hint of guilt that he was doing his duty, locking her up. Shell had planned the assault, which is why she stole the bottle from the party. It certainly does seem like malice aforethought on Shell's part; Karen just had to be sure. She also worries that Marilyn Fenner is still in love with Jim. He reassures her that he and Marilyn are just friends now, not letting on that he has given Marilyn hope that there's still a future for them.

Shell's life is being made a misery by Mad Tessa, who remembers how Shell tried to threaten her when she was admitted to G-Wing. Shell is forced to clean for and then sing for Tessa. When Shell can sing no more, she tries other forms of entertainment, treating Mad Tessa to some of her impressions. These do not go down well, bringing Tessa close to violence. Shell is desperate and goes into a tap-dancing routine. She finishes and awaits Tessa's wrath, but, instead, Tessa claps wildly and offers her a biscuit. When Sylvia comes in, hoping to find Shell beaten to a pulp, she discovers the two happily munching away. Time for Plan B.

Tessa's enthusiasm for Shell is growing into something akin to lust as she brushes her hair and makes her try on her old girlfriend, Debbie's, dress. The last straw for Shell is waking up to find Tessa in her bed. When Sylvia reappears, Shell begs her to let her go back to G-Wing. Cruelly, Sylvia gives her some hope, then takes her for her shower. Shell, more buoyant than she's been for some time, reaches for her towel after showering, but it's been removed by one of the inmates, Pamela Jolly. Pamela has been starved of her tranquilliser and she's been told that one person is to blame: Shell Dockley. Shell is beaten black and blue. Outside, Sylvia and Betty are delighted.

Helen's enquiry is going nowhere fast. She reluctantly comes to the conclusion that she may well have got Jim wrong and feels a little guilty. She was hardly being professional

when she slept with one of her prisoners and sneaked her back to Larkhall without informing the authorities. A breakthrough comes in the form of Yvonne Atkins. She tells Helen what she didn't know: that Jim and Karen are shagging. And, what's more, Yvonne reveals she shared this observation with Shell just before her attack on Jim. Meanwhile, on G1 landing, the two Julies are off to post their requests to Simon Stubberfield, hoping they'll be considered for electronic tagging. When Helen leads a bloodied Shell back to her cell on G3, Sylvia is gob-smacked. She sends a rallying cry to the troops – they're going on strike.

EPISODE 3 **SERIES 3**

Sylvia has been trying to negotiate with her union hierarchy to make her strike call legal, but she is told in no uncertain terms that it isn't. Only one thing for it, then, a mass 'sickie' where each prison officer will report in too ill to work.

Karen takes phone call after phone call and soon realises that she has no staff to work on the Wing. Understaffing means being banged up 24/7 for the women, but Helen suggests they allow the prisoners to organise themselves. Simon is wary – he's had one too many 'incidents' of late – but Karen is willing to give it a try, so long as Shell Dockley remains locked in her cell. The women are duly let out and Simon waits with baited breath for things to go wrong.

Karen makes every effort to convince Helen that her relationship with Jim has not affected her professional judgement of him. She tells Helen that, if she thought he'd raped Shell: 'I'd have his balls on a skewer'. Helen explains that Shell was terrified Karen's intimacy with Jim may have led to her telling the story of Shell's childhood abuse. Karen

seeks out Shell and assures her that she would never have revealed this.

Far away from the prisoner-managed G-Wing, Julie S., having won her case for electronic tagging, is ensconced in ex-inmate Monica's halfway house. She is, however, in turmoil, having left behind Julie J., whose request for tagging was turned down due to previous bad behaviour.

Julie S. is anxiously anticipating the arrival of a face from the past: her ex-boyfriend, Trevor, father to her son, David. Trevor turns out to be a modest, kind man and Julie S. feels old stirrings inside. They're clearly reciprocated by Trevor. Julie S. worries that Trevor will reject her if he knows about her past, so she and Monica initially present themselves as travel agents. Trevor is taken in, believing that Julie S. has done very well for herself with her fancy job and big house. Trevor's innocence stirs Julie S.'s conscience and she comes clean – she met Monica inside and she is nothing but a tart. Julie S. leaves him to ponder on that little lot, hoping against hope that he'll make the effort to come and see his son for the first time in his school play, *Macbeth*.

Things are going swimmingly on G-Wing with the prisoners in charge. In fact, the inmates are enjoying proving that it is far better run without the officers there. Then Yvonne makes a startling discovery: a kitchen knife has gone missing from the secure cabinet. This could ruin it for their self-run regime. She immediately suspects Shaz and

Denny, who have been standing in for the two Julies on cleaning duties. They complain loudly as their cell is 'spun' by Yvonne – they didn't take it. No one suspects Julie J., who is putting on a front to mask the deep depression she feels at Julie S.'s 'rejection' of her.

The officers' mass sickie continues but one officer is sicker than most: Di Barker. Di has learned that Dominic, the object of her bizarre fixation, is not returning to Larkhall, but is staying in Greece with someone he's met out there. The horror of the unrelenting drudgery of her life, looking after her bed-ridden mother, overwhelms her. She is teetering on the brink of a severe nervous breakdown and she responds to her mother's pleas for help by smacking her: 'You want me, now you've got me.'

Monica and Julie S. arrive at David's school, as planned. The play is just about to begin when Trevor makes an appearance. Julie S. fills up and there is a tender moment between them which might augur very well for a future relationship. However, that relationship is not to be. As Julie S. watches the famous dagger scene in *Macbeth*, something makes her feel very uneasy. She tries to dismiss it, but she just can't. She dashes from the assembly hall and runs in the direction of Larkhall prison. Julie S.'s hunch is right, Julie J. is in deep despair and prepares to end it all with the kitchen knife she's stolen.

Monica and Trevor catch up with Julie S. and are eventually persuaded to drive her to Larkhall. Julie S. pleads with Officer Blakeson to let her in, 'I've broke my curfew,' she tells

him. He slams the door in her face – it is a police matter.

Julie S. has no option: she takes control of Monica's car and drives it into the gate. The racket arouses the inmates who are gob-smacked that Julie S. is breaking into prison. 'What, is she mad or something?' Denny enquires of the prison population. Julie J.'s heart flips over – Julie S. has come back to her.

Meanwhile, behind the scenes, Simon has done a deal with Sylvia. Simon promises to reinstate her as a senior officer if she calls off her protest; Sylvia is nothing if not self-motivated. The halcyon days of self-rule are over for G-Wing.

EPISODE 4 SERIES 3

Barbara waits nervously for visiting time. Her late husband's children, Amanda and Greg, are to visit her for the first time. Nikki is intrigued, as she didn't think Barbara had any sort of relationship with them. Barbara explains this is why she's so nervous! Someone else at Larkhall is also expecting a visitor. Thanks to an old contact of Nikki's, a very sexually frustrated Yvonne has set up a rendezvous with a male prostitute who is posing as her lawyer. She tarts herself up and prepares for the liaison. However, Sylvia is suspicious. The prostitute, Guy, is nervous and, when Sylvia listens at the door of their interview room, she can hear nothing. 'If he's giving her legal advice, he's doing it in sign language,' she trumpets. She barges in but Yvonne has been too smart for her and everything appears as as it should be; Sylvia has been thwarted.

Meanwhile, Greg and Amanda turn up and make a shocking allegation: Barbara is a bigamist. They want the police to reinvestigate the death of their father, Peter. According to them, Barbara isn't a mercy killer who should be serving time for manslaughter: she's a cold-hearted, greedy murderer. Barbara is so offended that she smacks Greg hard across the face and is led back to her cell, to the sympathetic women on G-Wing.

G-Wing has been understaffed since Dominic's failure to return and a new female officer, Gina Rossi, reports for work. Gina is a loud-mouthed, sexually alluring woman, who has been transferred against her will from D-Wing owing to a fight with a prisoner over her boyfriend, Mark.

Di is depressed; Gina is no substitute for Dominic. She is in the depths of despair when Josh Mitchell offers some friendly words of advice: 'The best way to get over these things – find someone else and forget him.' It's advice that Josh is going to live to regret, as Di embarks on a plan to persuade him to join the prison service. Pretty soon, the name 'Dominic' is being scraped off her dressing room mirror, with the name 'Josh' substituted instead.

Back in Larkhall, Barbara continues to fret: what if she can't prove she was properly married to Peter? Will she be locked up for life? The women rally to her cause. They aim to grind Amanda and Greg down with constant phone calls and a letter campaign to 'persuade' them to abandon their hostilities against Barbara.

The women keep their plan a secret from Barbara and set about their task with gusto. Shell is particularly enthusiastic. There's nothing she likes better than a bit of terrorising and she makes all kinds of gruesome threats. 'You want to have kids one day, Amanda? 'Cos

if we cut your bits and pieces out, you won't be able to.' Naturally, the plan fails. As Denny shouts down the phone to Greg: 'You evil little wanker', she hasn't a clue that Karen has intercepted her call. Denny and Shaz are given extra days on their sentences but it's a price they're willing to pay to help Barbara out.

Sylvia's jaw sets when she discovers that Yvonne has got yet another legal visit. She knows that she's on to something and asks Karen's permission to investigate. Permission is granted. Sylvia brings Yvonne's 'lawyer', Ian Ravenscroft, into the interview room and goes off to alert the Dedicated Search Team to a major breach of security. What Sylvia doesn't know is that Ian is the genuine article. He is Charlie's lawyer and he's there to ask a favour from Yvonne: can she lie for Charlie in court? Before Yvonne can answer, Sylvia bursts in with her DST colleagues and orders a personal search. When it's clear that Sylvia has made an error of gargantuan proportions, she withdraws, blaming the DST for her mistake. Ian eventually leaves with Yvonne's agreement – she will do what Charlie wants.

Things on G1 aren't going well for Barbara. She is called to Karen's office where two police officers await. They accuse her of bigamy and tell they're going to reopen their investigation. She returns to her cell and admits that she has been lying to Nikki and the other women all along. She is a bigamist, but she insists she married Peter for all the right reasons. Her staunch Catholic husband was trying to thwart her and wouldn't agree to a divorce; it was all they could do. Nikki and the other women are disgusted – after all they've done for her.

Matters are made worse when Sylvia reveals that Barbara has inherited millions – another fact that she has concealed. Barbara is humiliated and mortified in equal measure. Nikki takes pity on her and suggests a way of getting back into the women's good books. Not long afterwards, Barbara makes a phone call to Monica and tells the women of G-Wing that there's going to be another half-way house, courtesy of Barbara's inheritance. Reconciliation is in the air.

EPISODE 5 SERIES 3

There is amazement on G-Wing when news gets out that Yvonne is willing to testify for her husband in court. Yvonne retains a sphinx-like silence, but she is more forthcoming to her daughter, Lauren: 'You're young, love. There is more goes on in a marriage than you know. Some ties can't be broken.' Lauren wants Yvonne to dump her father right in it, but Yvonne claims she is not going to do that. Lauren leaves, disgusted with her mother.

Another prison sweat-box sweeps into Larkhall, carrying seventeen-year-old smackhead Buki Lester in it. Buki is multi-pierced and mouthy with it, and she joins Shaz and Denny in the four-bed dorm. It quickly becomes clear that Buki is a boastful, compulsive liar –

especially where her self-piercings are concerned. Shaz is wide-eyed with wonder as Buki shows the girls her tongue stud: 'I only got earrings, man.'

Jim returns to duty, joining the other staff back on G-Wing. He is clearly anxious about what might await him, and Shell loses no time in making him feel very uncomfortable indeed.

Josh has been pondering long and hard about what Di has said to him about joining the prison service. She is delighted when he tells her he thinks he'll give it a go. Di is elated that her plan has worked. Like Dominic before him, Josh now has a dedicated shrine in her bedroom at home, and a shrine needs objects to worship. The first thing Di purloins is Josh's bandana. As luck would have it for Shaz, Di doesn't realise there is a nail stuck in it. When Di takes the bandana from her pocket to have a little feel, the nail falls to the floor and Shaz swipes it.

Shaz takes the nail back to Denny, with a spring in her step. Here is an object that will allow them to pierce their own tongues! Denny balks, immediately coming up with several excuses as to why that isn't such a good idea. But Shaz is insistent and, under her pressure, Denny is forced to give way. Shaz gathers together the equipment for the job: ice, an apple, alcohol and sharpened nail. Denny sticks her tongue out for the piercing with trepidation. Major mistake – Shaz wasn't to know that she would pierce an artery! Denny heads for bed in agony, her swollen tongue occupying all the available space in her mouth. Buki's words ring in her ears – she didn't do her tongue herself: 'Got that done professional.'

The next day, Yvonne is up early, waiting for Sylvia and Gina to escort her to court, for her to testify. Back down on G1, Denny isn't stirring; in fact she has lost consciousness.

Shaz wakes to find Denny's pillow covered in blood. The doctor is called and all hell breaks loose. Shaz is distraught, believing that she has killed Denny. Karen orders a cell spin to find the nail, but it has gone. Yvonne has secretly and helpfully removed it. As Denny heads for hospital, Yvonne heads for court, her heart still apparently set on lying for Charlie.

At the court, Yvonne blows a kiss to Charlie and takes her place on the stand. When the prosecuting counsel asks her what the packages delivered to her home contained, Yvonne tells him straight that she knew they contained Charlie's drugs: 'Charlie told me to watch out for them.'

It becomes clear that Yvonne is not out to support Charlie but to dump him right in it. There ensues much legal wrangling, with Charlie insisting that his only hope is to take the stand. His lawyer reluctantly agrees. Their strategy is simple: make out that Yvonne, a wronged, jealous woman is out to get her own back on him for his affair with Renee Williams. They paint a picture of Yvonne as evil and scheming and make much of the fact that her address is HMP Larkhall.

When the jury returns with their verdict, Yvonne is horrified to learn that Charlie is found not guilty of the most serious charge and is free to walk from court. With his blonde-

haired moll on his arm, Charlie makes a nice little speech from the steps of the court about Great British justice. Yvonne, hand-cuffed to Gina and Sylvia, passes by and curses him. But she is interrupted by a pizza delivery man, who gets off his scooter, opens his pizza box, pulls out a gun and shoots Charlie right in the forehead. It takes Yvonne only a few seconds to realise that Lauren is responsible.

Meanwhile, Shaz is horrified to learn that Denny might have blood poisoning and that her life is hanging in the balance. But it is not all doom and gloom on the Wing – certainly not for Di Barker. Josh tells Di that he has passed his test for the prison service and she dreams of their having a long and happy relationship together.

EPISODE 6 SERIES 3

Helen surprises everyone when she brings a psychiatric unit inmate (and erstwhile arsonist) onto the Lifers' Unit. Pamela 'Podger' Jolly has already met Shell, having attacked her in the Muppet Wing showers, and Shell is scared. Jim, still struggling with the after-effects of 'Shell' shock, is also frightened – another psycho on the Wing! He complains to Karen, who tells him she is tired of his anti-Helen rants. Jim plays for sympathy, suggesting that perhaps Shell's attack has made him more sensitive than usual. Karen warms to this idea; a lesser man would have left the service long ago.

The two Julies discover a little cat in the prison grounds, and call him Tinker. They hide him in their cell, until he is nearly discovered while Di shows trainee prison officer Josh Mitchell the ropes. Josh is on his induction fortnight and there is some gentle banter with him from the inmates, until Di jealously tells him to watch out for sexual advances. The Julies realise they can't keep Tinker in their cell, so they persuade a reluctant Nikki to let him stay in her potting shed.

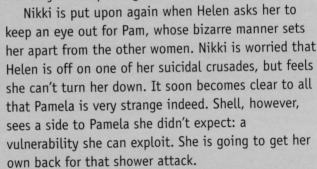

Nikki is put upon again when Helen asks her to keep an eye out for Pam, whose bizarre manner sets her apart from the other women. Nikki is worried that Helen is off on one of her suicidal crusades, but feels she can't turn her down. It soon becomes clear to all that Pamela is very strange indeed. Shell, however, sees a side to Pamela she didn't expect: a vulnerability she can exploit. She is going to get her own back for that shower attack.

Meanwhile, Helen arranges for Shaz to visit a recovering Denny in the prison hospital. Denny makes it clear that she bears no grudges and she'll be back on the Wing in a couple of weeks. Shaz is more relieved than she can say.

Shell sets about making Pamela's life a misery. She humiliates her in front of the inmates, but she's got something even better up her sleeve; she plans to exploit Pamela's past history and also do the dirty on her arch-enemy, Nikki Wade. Shell proceeds to light a nice little pyre of Nikki's books, including her precious copy of *Sophie's World*, the first thing Helen gave her.

Pamela is at once blamed, just as Shell planned. Everyone puts pressure on Helen, including Nikki: 'I warned you not to bring that fat headcase up here. But you always know best, don't you?' Something about Pamela disturbs Helen greatly and she demands that Dr Nicholson explain his diagnosis of Pamela as a 'manic depressive'. Dr Nicholson is defensive and then admits that neither he, nor his staff, have any psychiatric training.

Down in the potting shed, Tinker has gone missing, Shell gains more amusement from

pinning the blame on Pamela: 'I heard a cat sound through the wall...Don't go by me, but she could stuff anything up that tent dress.' The Julies wouldn't normally believe Shell, but they've already seen Pamela kick out in horror at Tinker. When the Julies and their posse challenge Pamela about it, she just smiles at them, so both she and her cell are smashed up.

Karen is at the end of her tether and the clock is ticking for Pamela's stay on G-Wing. Helen has to act fast. It doesn't take long for a psychiatrist, Dr Thomas Waugh, to realise that he is dealing with a paranoid schizophrenic in Pamela and he prescribes anti-psychotic drugs and talk therapies. He also questions Nicholson's competence – it was impossible that he couldn't have spotted Pamela's delusional symptoms. Helen could kiss Dr Waugh in gratitude, and it's clear he wouldn't resist this.

Shaz makes an indiscreet remark to Josh about Crystal. Josh tries to laugh it off, as he has been warned by Crystal to keep their relationship a secret. The ever-hovering Di is nevertheless suspicious and quizzes Shaz, who replies: 'Everyone knows about him fancying Crystal.' Di resolves to put a stop to this. She lets Josh know that Crystal is the number one suspect in the theft of Sylvia's clock. Josh is shocked and hurt. When Denny returns to the Wing, Josh seeks her out and asks her to be straight with him: did Crystal nick the clock? Denny covers for Crystal and denies this, much to Josh's relief.

Meanwhile, Dr Waugh's regime is beginning, slowly but surely, to have an effect on Pamela. His professional judgement about her previous medical treatment propels Simon Stubberfield to request Dr Nicholson's resignation.

The Julies come out of mourning Tinker's demise when Nikki takes them to see 'his' return as a new mother with a litter of kittens. Nikki seeks Helen out and asks her to: 'sign a release warrant' for Tinkerbell and family. Helen is pleased to oblige, then remembers that she has a gift for Nikki: a new copy of *Sophie's World*, with a personal message inside.

Jim remains cowed and nervous when he is anywhere near Shell. In a move designed to frighten the life out of him, she unfurls a bloody sheet in his face. Jim nearly faints, all the horrors of his attack returning. The one person he blames for all this is Helen Stewart, and he sexually assaults her in the P.O.'s office. A few miles away, outside Josh and Crystal's home in Acton, another sexual predator lurks: Di Barker.

EPISODE 7 · SERIES 3

The officers are told that a television documentary team, Kicking Productions, will be using Larkhall to shoot a fly-on-the-wall documentary. There is consternation among the staff, voiced by Sylvia: 'Like we haven't got enough to do without entertaining the nation to boot.' Karen makes it clear that no one will be filmed without their consent. It is clear that she's not particularly happy about this herself; however, Simon Stubberfield sees it as good PR.

Helen, meanwhile, is in a terrible dilemma: she has no idea what to do about Jim's assault on her. She can't prove it and no one will believe her because of their past feuding. She is in a deeper predicament when she discovers that Karen is considering moving in with Jim. Helen turns to Nikki, who is horrified at what he's done: 'I'll kill him.' Helen swears Nikki to silence. Nikki promises, but it is clear that what she promises and what she'll do are two different things. Jim tracks Helen down; he is prepared to apologise and blames the trauma on Shell's assault. Helen doesn't buy this, calling him a 'piece of shit'. Jim covers his tracks, telling Karen he is worried Helen has a vendetta against him. He goes so far as

to suggest that she might invent a sexual assault. Karen dismisses the notion but assures Jim that, should such an outrageous thing happen, she'll be there for him. Job done.

Kicking Productions arrives at Larkhall and proceeds to capture the routines of prison life on film. Many prisoners and prison officers, despite their protestations, have done themselves up for the camera. Sylvia sports a new hairdo and Shell has donned extra-sexy gear. The first shot the director, Fiona, wants is Simon walking onto the Wing and being greeted by the women. Things don't quite go according to plan, though, as he is met with blank faces: 'Who's he?' Buki asks. Shaz doesn't know: 'Stubber-something,' she replies. Fiona is forced to cut and reshoot.

Shell is thrilled to be interviewed about her case, especially since it's a chance to proclaim her innocence. Sound man, Chris, stands close by. Shell has taken a shine to Chris and has picked up a little hint of something (pheromones?) from him. Prompted by Fiona, Shell goes into every gory detail of her victim's torture and demise. She doesn't know that, outside, Jim is listening in, the sweat forming on his brow. Shell uses the opportunity of an audience to bang on about the indignities of prison life – particularly the fact that male officers can get into the women's cells any time of the day or night. She is just about to tell the film crew about Jim Fenner, when Jim steels himself to enter her cell and terminate the interview. He is shaking, his stomach is churning and he is forced to make a hasty exit. Jim is losing it and something is going to have to give.

Meanwhile, Buki is playing up to the camera and we see just what a disturbed young woman she really is. She cuts herself up and Fiona manages to get her wired for sound while Simon plays the caring Governing Governor. Things don't go according to plan, however, as Buki humiliates Simon when she gets the best of the verbal exchange. Simon decides that only his words will be recorded for the viewers, and Buki's logical interventions will be cut. Fiona is annoyed, but not as annoyed as Julie S. is, when she discovers that she has to sign a disclaimer form agreeing to her son being filmed for the nation, or she won't get a visit. Gina is angry, too, about Fiona lording it over the officers. Helen becomes furious when the camera crew crashes into her Lifers' meeting. The only person who seems to be wallowing in the crew's presence is Shell, who is developing a flirtatious relationship with Chris.

Jim's mind goes into overdrive; there is something he can exploit here. With great difficulty, he faces Shell and tells her he has a plan to allow her to escape. She is cynical at first, but he persuades her that he is genuine. He wants her out and part of his plan includes pointing the finger at Helen. Jim makes an impression of the film crew's van key and of his own gate and door keys. He tapes them to a prison church pew and tells Shell exactly where to look. Of course, he warns her, no one must know. Of course, she ignores him and blabs to Denny, telling her that she's coming too. Denny is reluctant, as she

doesn't want to leave Shaz. But Shaz can solve that problem – she can come along too!

The last hymn is being sung in church. On cue, Julie S. creates the diversion Shell needs when she slaps Chris's sound pole out of his hands. In the melee, Shell makes her escape, followed by Denny, followed, to Shell's irritation, by Shaz. They get into the van as planned and drive out of Larkhall. Shell's impatience, however, causes her to stall the van and all three are forced to make a run for it. Shaz hurts her ankle as she jumps from the van, but she encourages Denny to go on without her. Shell and Denny catch a cab and head for King's Cross and a new life.

Meanwhile, Jim is in a panic. Three prisoners have escaped. The police are going to be crawling all over the place for them. He is in, as he would say himself, 'deep shit'.

Dutch Courage
– SHED: The Beginning

Were it not for the unreliability of Britain's railways, *Bad Girls* may never have got beyond the stage of being an intriguing idea. Had the train that Brian Park, Ann McManus and Eileen Gallagher taken from Manchester to London in August1997 not been delayed, Shell and Fenner, Helen and Nikki, Bodybag and Dominic might never have become flesh, blood and bone. Let us give thanks, then, for the unpredictability of the nation's railways. That, and the inspirational effects of red wine.

Never ones to be confined by conventions or hemmed in by expectations – never mind railway timetables – it is perhaps apt that the trio were stuck, friends on a train, when they came up with the idea for *Bad Girls* and the courage to start their own production company. Park, then the producer of *Coronation Street*, McManus, the soap's script executive, and Gallagher, the managing director of LWT, had no reason whatsoever to embark upon such an uncertain venture. Their respective jobs were high-flying, high-profile and high-paying positions.

Gallagher had worked her way up from press officer at Scottish Television through the ranks at Granada and eventually to managing director of LWT. Park may have made his name as the axeman of Coronation Street but he had been a TV producer for years, having worked on the award-winning *Prime Suspect IV* as well as countless others over a twenty-year career. McManus, meanwhile, had masterminded Deirdre's pilot error and subsequent jail term in *Coronation Street*, after many years of writing for some of television's best-loved soaps.

Of course, it wasn't just dutch courage that inspired Shed Productions. After years at the top of the TV industry, they had all become frustrated with working on other people's dramas rather than their own. The new production team was not complete, however, without a top writer. No discussion was needed. Maureen Chadwick, known as 'Chad', was a close colleague and star writer on *Coronation Street*. Conveniently, Chadwick had also written a screenplay based on the youthful criminal career of the now famous women prisoners' rights campaigner, Chris Tchaikovsky. The four friends had previously discussed the possibility of a series set in a women's prison. The dramatic potential was obvious. So also was the opportunity of highlighting the abuses and absurdities of a prison system that wastes so many, often already abused, women's lives – and those of their dependent children.

But would ITV go for *Jailbirds*, as it was then called, or would they think it too risky, too risqué and too *Prisoner: Cell Block H* to take a chance? It wasn't a cosy medical drama or a life-affirming police show; it was dark, difficult, deliciously dangerous drama – never mind the odds against ITV handing a big commission to an independent production company rather than to one of its constituent companies, like Granada or Carlton. A meeting with Nick Elliott and Jenny Reeks, controllers of drama at ITV's Network Centre, went exceptionally well. They were so impressed they asked for ten episodes instead of the eight they had planned for. They also promised it would be shown at 9 p.m., the most coveted slot for a drama on ITV. With that news, the Shed team cracked open the Champagne and handed in their resignations.

Shed were, however, soon to learn that this was by no means the end of the commissioning process. ITV soon clarified their own position, a move which highlighted the precariousness of Shed's: the green light would only be given when the first script was delivered – and only if it was acceptable. The Shed team had no jobs, no money and, as yet, no commission.

The spotlight turned on Chad. 'We locked her in a secure room,' jokes Gallagher,' and didn't let her out until the script was finished.' Four weeks later, she emerged with her work. Park, McManus and Gallagher were delighted, as was ITV when the script was delivered to them. The commission was officially Shed's.

Then the really hard work started. While ITV was supportive, it is standard practice for a production company not to get paid until the completed series is delivered. For Shed, finding the money to build sets, pay actors, scriptwriters and the crew – not to mention shelling out for film stock, the cameras themselves, post-production, editors and edit suites, make-up, costumes and catering – was more of a problem. For the ten-part *Bad Girls*, five million pounds would have to be raised. Unfortunately, as a newly-formed, virginal independent company, Shed didn't have much of a credit rating. In fact, it didn't have one at all.

Short of selling half their company to investors and putting their homes up as collateral, received wisdom dictated that there was no way the Shed team could raise the necessary funds. Understandably, they weren't keen to take such a drastic course of action, especially as it meant giving up ownership of their 'baby' before it was even a toddler – and, were Shed to fail, losing their homes to boot.

Ever the down-to-earth mavericks, Park, McManus, Gallagher and Chadwick did what the rest of us do when we want a loan: they went to the bank. Even for the media specialist Barclays Bank in Soho, a five-million-pound loan to a completely unknown company was a tall order. However, they liked the sound of *Bad Girls* and the talent behind it, and the team walked out five million pounds richer. Not that they were allowed to spend the money on anything but *Bad Girls* ...

With the money in their pockets, the producer could start hiring crew, checking actors' availability and imagining HMP Larkhall. But before any of that could happen, the scripts had to be right. From the outset, Shed sought to break the conventions of British drama and instead adopt a more American style of working, providing detailed storylines for writers who would then create dialogue. In the early days of production, some of the writers the team had taken a gamble on were terrific, while others weren't so promising. A couple of the scripts had to be rewritten against the clock to meet the high standards exacted by Park, McManus, Gallagher and Chadwick. With the script factory up and running, work could now begin on the production.

After much discussion, Shed decided to build their own set rather than film in an existing prison. That decision cost them some five hundred thousand pounds, although few would argue that it hasn't paid off. With the casting also complete, Shed had a Christmas party to introduce the cast to each other and to the whole Shed team. 'As they walked into the room,' Gallagher recalls, 'I could guess which characters were which. Brian had found our Shell, Jim, Helen, Nikki and I felt like I knew them, and everyone else, immediately and intimately.' And luckily, everyone hit it off.

Shooting took twenty-eight weeks, during which time Park – who was on set virtually

every day – took progress reports and rough edits back to the rest of the Shed team. Over nearly two hundred days, Larkhall, its inmates and staff began to take shape. As they did so, ten hours of drama, the first series of *Bad Girls*, was created.

The Shed team knew *Bad Girls* was a series they loved, exactly the series they set out to make. It was something different from anything else on prime-time British television, with its daring combination of hard-hitting female-centred stories, initially often unsympathetic characters and humour. All that remained was to see whether ITV's head honchos and, more importantly, the public would share their enthusiasm. When the first episode was screened on May 8th, 1998, Brian Park, Ann McManus, Eileen Gallagher and Maureen Chadwick sat down to watch it with the rest of the UK, each with a glass of red wine in hand...

Where the Buck Stops
– The Directors

Keeping a large cast and crew in check as well as filming an hour's worth of drama in little over two weeks is a tall order. New characters need new actors to bring them alive. How are over fifty scenes going to be shot and in what order? What car would Di's mother have sitting idly in her drive? What wallpaper would adorn Josh's flat? Would Shell's mother boast this shade of blue eyeshadow?

So many questions... and the person responsible for pulling together the right answers is the director. Of course, the director has a huge group of experienced and talented crew members to help build the alternate world of a women's prison and its inhabitants. But the buck stops at the director's door.

Fortunately, *Bad Girls* has a great line-up of trusted directors who have contributed much to the programme. Mike Adams, Laurence Moody and Jim O'Hanlon and, latterly, Jo Johnson have taken up the gauntlet and delivered episode after episode of *Bad Girls*.

'Basically, the first thing you do is rewrite the script in your head – in pictures,' Jim O'Hanlon explains. The script is broken down, scene by scene, and decisions are made as to how and in what order to shoot it. Every minute detail is planned, with locations scouted and new characters cast. We have meetings with the design, costume and make-up departments and generally get as much sorted out as possible before filming starts. That's when things get a little hectic,' Jim laughs.

Some scenes demand advance rehearsal but, otherwise, there is just a five-minute artiste dry run. The crew also has a camera rehearsal to ensure that lighting and sound are in order. The process is lengthy and intensive. About a month is spent planning and plotting in pre-production, then there's approximately a month of filming two episodes simultaneously and then up to eight weeks in the editing room doing post-production.

Mike explains how he entered the *Bad Girls* universe as the first director on the first show of the first series: 'Filming the first episode demanded establishing the characters almost immediately. The fashion show was ideal. It was a great opener and introduced us to many of the personalities. The overall goal has remained the same since the start anyway: to tell the stories in the clearest and most engaging way to the audience. Besides, female characters are just more interesting, I think.'

So, with several directors, how does the show maintain its seamless edge? Jim comments: 'Well, obviously we have the same cast and crew. But I also think that, whilst each of us directors has individual strengths, we share a common vision'. Mike smiles and adds: 'I want to see the characters evolve in the audience's perception, provide lots of surprises and, basically, tell a good story. We want to represent real prison life, or, as I see it, real life with the dull bits left out!'

Fertile Territory –
The Creation of *Bad Girls*

Shed knew it had fertile territory for drama in the unusual situation of a closed world where one set of human beings locks up another set for a living.

It would be eye-level entertainment grounded in fact: drama with a heart and a conscience. But the huge task of turning the idea into compelling characters and stories had to be accomplished against the clock, so Chad, Eileen and Ann sentenced themselves to fourteen days' hard labour – in the confinement of a Tuscan villa. (Brian had to stay at home finishing his tenure as *Coronation Street* producer.)

The team struggled on to a plane, loaded down with research material. Once safely in Italy, Eileen remembers coming down to the dining room for her first meal: 'It was like a reference library,' she laughs. 'Piles of academic books, old copies of the Prison Officers' magazine *Gate Lodge*, prisoners' autobiographies, photographs of Victorian jails ...'

Each day began at 9 a.m. sharp, with an intensive reading session, followed by discussion and debate about the kind of characters who would populate their prison world. Chad remembers: 'We wanted characters who represented a range of ages, backgrounds and attitudes, but each with a fully rounded personality and a distinctive voice'. Each character was written on a piece of paper, put into a hat (actually, a salad bowl) and a lucky dip determined who would name and shape them. 'You know you've got a real character when you find yourself saying: "Lorna Rose wouldn't do that,"' laughs Eileen.

With a roster of personalities lined up, the next job was to plot the major storylines they wanted to cover. The trio had agreed that the drama would focus on one Wing, run by an idealistic young woman governor, and that there would be two major officer/inmate relationships at its core. 'We wanted to do a classic forbidden love story that would span the entire series,' Eileen recalls.

In Helen Stewart, Shed's aim was to create a heroine who failed – at least some of the time. Helen doesn't wave a magic wand and sort out everyone's problems for them. In fact, many of her problems are of her own making. 'To complicate matters for her,' says Chad, 'we created an intelligent, highly political prisoner in Nikki Wade – who loathes anyone who works in prisons – and a devious, misogynistic senior officer, Jim Fenner, who hates fast-track idealists who think they know it all.'

The presence of male officers in women's prisons (thanks to equal opportunities legislation) is something that shocked the *Bad Girls* team. They came across scores of hitherto untold inmates' stories of sexual intimidation and abuse. The Jim Fenner/Shell Dockley relationship was to illustrate the complex potential of this situation, while the story of Rachel Hicks was to show its full horror.

Another outrage Shed was determined to highlight was how the imprisonment of women often punishes whole families by separating mothers from their children. They chose an unusual angle through which to dramatise this: the story of Monica and her son, Spencer, a man in his thirties with Down's Syndrome. Monica's extreme reaction at Spencer's funeral, when she jumps into his grave after being uncuffed from Helen, was based on a true story told to the team by a retired prison governor.

The next stage in the creation of *Bad Girls* was the construction of Larkhall prison. Brian explains,' I wanted to have an old Victorian-style prison. Architecturally, it's like a cathedral with lots of atmosphere and mood. It creates a formidable sort of reality, with stark, fluorescent lighting and claustrophobic shadows.'

Casting the characters was the next challenge. Along with Judy Hayfield and, later, Margaret Crawford, Brian assembled a huge ensemble cast. Brian points out: 'We needed people who could hit the ground running. All we gave them was a paltry page of script and told them to improvise the rest. We knew that all of the characters would evolve so much, the actors would need the range and instincts not only to evolve with them but also to help inform their development. Luckily we were able to find a great cast – many of whom are relative newcomers to television as well – which is very satisfying.'

As Brian set about casting, the daunting task of writing was also confronted: constructing and scripting ten episodes. All the storylines and scripts for the first series were written before the very first episode was broadcast. 'We wanted to end the series, which for all we knew would be the end of the drama altogether, with a bang. Actually, several bangs,' says Chad. 'We had come so far with Helen and Nikki, but we still felt there was a rich vein to mine.' adds Ann. 'We wanted our audience to be shouting at the screen: "No! You can't leave them like that!"'

The first few weeks on air were scary times for Shed. They watched the ratings for the first few episodes dip and read the host of vicious reviews. Then, suddenly, it all began to turn around ... *Bad Girls* is now in its third series and is a major success story. It has won several major TV drama awards, is sold round the world and has a loyal following of fantastic fans. The task of turning several pages of ideas into living, breathing characters has been accomplished, and there's no turning back.

Heavy Steel – The Building of Larkhall

Stepping on to the set of *Bad Girls* is an awesome experience. It is said to be the biggest free-standing television set in Europe. The prison gates are forged from heavy steel and the atmosphere is totally authentic. So authentic, in fact, that when ex-prisoners have visited they feel they're doing time again. Understandably, they usually don't hang around for too long!

The man behind the UK's newest Victorian prison is Mike Oxley, Shed's first production designer responsible for the original design and build. From the earliest days, the series creators had decided Larkhall had to be an older Victorian prison rather than the more modern designs being built today. Oxley and director Mike Adams found the

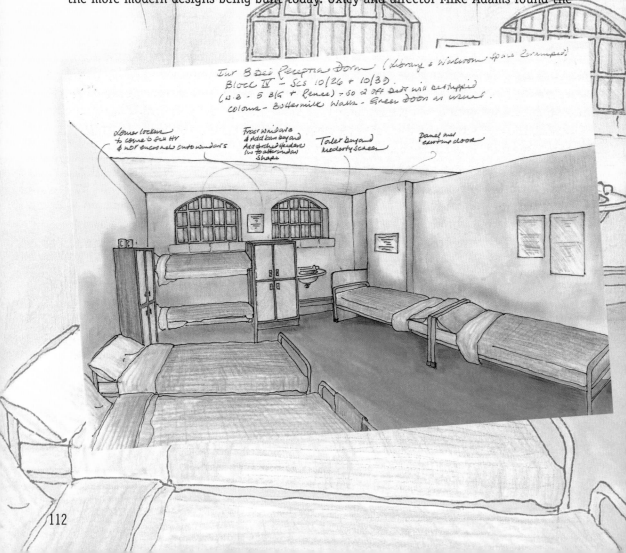

perfect model in Oxford Prison, the interior of which was the basis for Larkhall's G-Wing, from the shape of the cell doors to the huge window that dominates the landing. The distinctive colour scheme of buttermilk and green was also copied from Oxford, then modified to get the right look for the camera.

The core of the set is a massive, heavy metal structure. Jane Tomblin, the production designer on later series of *Bad Girls*, supervised the build of the original set with Oxley. She explains: 'We had to have a very robust three-storey structure, on which full camera and lighting crews could shoot half a dozen actors in perfect safety. That's a lot of weight and activity, so the structure had to be as sound as any in a real prison. That's partly what gives it such an authentic look.'

But authenticity comes as much from minute details as from the structure itself. The key to these all-important details is thorough research. The art department at Shed spent many weeks collecting detailed information from prisons around the country. The notices on G-Wing, such as: 'Please don't use the floor as an ashtray. It kills the cockroaches', are all copied from originals in prisons such as Winchester or Holloway. Just as in Larkhall, in any cell in a real prison you'll find noticeboards crammed with personal photographs and 'good luck' cards stuck on with toothpaste (pins, etc are banned).

As working prisons ban most photography, the art team had to rely on notes and drawings. Art Director Sally Reynolds recalls, 'At first, some prison authorities were quite helpful, letting us see official stationery, forms and the like, or prison-issue bags, so we could make authentic mock-ups of them. It's a bit more difficult now that the drama's on air and causing controversy.'

The design of Larkhall certainly doesn't end with the initial creation of a set and its dressings. Throughout the production, rooms in the admin. block are changed around -- in some cases, endlessly. Tomblin explains: 'The stage is full, so every room becomes seven or eight different sets. The library, the workroom, the eight-bed reception dorm and the art room are all just one room. Just by changing the shape of the window, the doors, the colour of the walls or adding a cupboard, you can make it look like a different room.'

Every bit of action requires particular props and dressings. In Helen's drawer, for example, you'll find Nikki's file complete with mugshot and hand-written notes relating, often, to the particular story being shot. Even if the camera can't pick out such details, they are all there to add to an authentic feeling on set.

The attention to detail is particularly important for *Bad Girls*. Tomblin explains: 'This is quite a difficult show to do. There are certain things you can and can't have in prisons and procedures and papers have to be right. If we don't get it right, there's plenty of people who have been in prison who will tell us! That's why I need, and have, one of the best teams around.'

Long Johns and Thermal Vests – Secrets from Behind the Scenes

Lindsey Fawcett gives a taste of life as a Bad Girls *cast member.*

When we arrive, at whatever ungodly hour, looking as though we've had about four hours sleep (which is often true!), we get into costume and head for Make-up. This place can work magic … if you haven't had enough sleep, you can take a little nap in the make-up chair and, it's amazing, you wake up looking fabulous!

If we're in first thing, we get given breakfast. This is brought up to Make-up by our runner, Debbie. Her job is to make sure we're all in the right place at the right time and that we don't wander off anywhere. She also keeps us updated on where we are in the

schedule and lets us know about any changes to the daily call sheet. Debbie always knows what's going on, as she's in constant radio contact with Wardrobe, Make-up, Props, the first, second and third A.D.s (Assistant Directors) and the rest of the crew. Oh, and she's really nice and gets us coffee and gives free massages. Ow! Stop twisting my arm now, Debbie – it hurts!

The make-up room is definitely the place to be at the studio. We do, however, also have a greenroom, and people use this to sleep on the sofas and watch TV between scenes. But, in the morning, most people congregate in Make-up for the social aspect (and, more importantly, the toaster!).

My favourite part of *Bad Girls* make-up is the blood and bruises. Whenever actors do a scene in which their character has been beaten up or cut in some way, it is the people in Make-up who create the carnage. In the scene in series 2, episode 12, when Mandana, as Nikki, stabs herself in the hand with a gardening fork, a combination of specialist make-up and 'reverse playback' were used to create the effect. Reverse playback is, according to director Lawrence Moody: 'one of the oldest tricks in the book'. Basically, the stunt is shot back to front, so that when it's played (backwards), it looks the right way round. Confused? What happened in the scene was Mandana started with a rubber fork pressed into her hand, she flinched and then pulled it out. This was played backwards to create the effect of her stabbing herself and then flinching with pain.

Reverse playback was also used when Julie S. tried to break into Larkhall after her release and tagging. The shot started with the car parked against the guard's legs. The stunt driver then reversed all the way out; again, the viewers saw this played backwards.

The technique is often used on very fast or dangerous stunts – well, we can't have P.O.s wandering around with broken legs or actresses with holes in their hands, can we?

Another great hang-out place at the studio is the stage door; this is the main entry to the set. I'm not sure why this is a place people are attracted to, as it's freezing cold and there's nowhere to sit (unless you count the metal steps on the props van). This is where our company nurse, the lovely Heather, is usually to be found. As well as attending to the sick and dying on set, Heather is a consultant for medical storylines and, occasionally, a background prisoner. If anyone needs a paracetamol, vitamin C, plaster, or hug, Heather is the woman to see. As is the case with practically everyone who works on *Bad Girls*, Heather is fab. Ow, that's the same arm that Debbie just twisted!

The props van is pretty impressive. The two geezers in charge are Bob and Ron. They sort out everything from making the lovely prison food to setting up the balls on the pool table; the Art Department and Props Department are responsible for making the set look real. Anything from photos on noticeboards to deodorant on lockers, to painting the doors the right shade of (lovely) green: these guys can do it.

Once we're on set, before filming a scene, we do a line-run rehearsal of the scene. This is our chance to work out with the director exactly when and where we need to move, and how to play the dialogue. When this is done, we have to clear out of the way while the lighting is set up and the camera brought in. This is usually an ideal opportunity to do a bit more hanging around by the stage door; there are tea and coffee urns there, so that keeps most of us happy.

After several years of waiting, Debbie will get a call on her radio receiver, to bring us back on to the set. I've usually forgotten all my lines by then, so it's lucky that we get to do a few more rehearsals! The director takes a first look on camera and there are normally a few more lighting tweaks to be done – more waiting. When we're finally ready to go for a take, Make-up and Wardrobe are called in to do checks and make sure we still look like we're supposed to. After a couple of *It'll Be Alright on the Night* moments, a few more lighting changes and camera moves, and several hours hanging around drinking tea, we have a completed scene. Then it's back to Wardrobe to change for the next scene and repeat the whole process again.

See, it's not all as glamorous as you might think. For example, it's so cold on set that most of us wear long johns and thermal vests under our costumes. Now there's a little-known secret! We do have a lot of fun, though. Everyone gets on with each other and we have a great laugh on set. I think, for me, the best part of this job is the people; the cast and crew are fab and I'm sure this fantastic work atmosphere is what makes *Bad Girls* such a top show.

A Real Solitary Cell –
A Visit to HMP Bullwood Hall

By Lyndsey Fawcett

My visit to Bullwood Hall was one of the strangest days of my life. From approaching the prison, set in beautiful grounds, to passing through the hefty gates where we were searched, to entering the prison itself – it was an experience that no amount of time in Larkhall could have prepared me for.

I arrived in a car with Alicya Eyo and Mandana Jones. We all became quite nervous as we approached the gates, and suddenly went very quiet. Even Mandana managed to shut her gob for a minute or two (joking!). A prison officer let us in through a door in the gate and checked our names and ID with their list. They rub-down searched us and checked our bags and pockets. We were advised to leave phones and wallets with them, as 'they'd almost certainly be nicked'. Although I was expecting it, having the door locked behind us seemed completely bizarre. Literally, every ten steps we took, there would be another gate to negotiate.

First of all we were taken to the gym, where there was a health fair going on. There were a few really young looking girls sitting outside with an officer. One of them spotted us and said 'Oh my god it's them from *Bad Girls* – Miss, I thought you were kidding about them coming!' She was really excited and started yelling that she was on G-Wing and a real *Bad Girl*. I'd been secretly hoping that they hadn't seen the show in case they didn't like it, so that was a really encouraging moment.

We braced ourselves and then strode into the gym (Alicya first – she's the bravest). We split up (a daring move) and wandered around the stalls. About twenty girls eventually found us and asked for autographs. I managed to speak to a few of them and was amazed at how young some of them were. The ones who approached me were very friendly and very excited about the next series. One girl joked that she'd offer me a cup of tea but ... which was really sweet and touching and sad at the same time. There were a lot of moments like that when I would be having a laugh with people and then suddenly realise that I was free to go whenever I wanted and they'd still be stuck in there.

One thing that really surprised me was the amount of self-harm going on. The sheer number of people with cutting-up scars was quite disturbing. It made me so angry that these women were locked up (mostly for petty crimes) with this huge lack of self-worth when most of them needed help and were a danger only to themselves.

Another thing I noticed was the huge amount of physical contact between inmates – but mostly girls with arms around each other in a kind of supportive and friendly way (though in some cases there was clearly more to it). I also saw one or two Shell Dockley outfits; that made me feel very at home!

We had lunch with the P.O.s and got to chat to a few of them. One guy got talking about the storylines in the programme. He said that during his career he had met doppelgangers of every P.O. in *Bad Girls*, even Bodybag! Mandana asked a female P.O. about the drug situation. Basically, before mandatory testing came in, the most widely used drug in Bullwood Hall was cannabis. However, as cannabis stays in the system for several weeks, many prisoners had begun to use

BULLWOOD HALL

heroin as an alternative as it leaves the body system quicker.

After lunch, we went to the fashion department, where inmates could do courses in design. They had recently done a fashion show that had won the prison an award, so this was a place that everyone was very proud of. There were about six dresses on dummies that were gorgeous – I think Mandana was thinking about nicking one of them! The tutor told us about one of the inmates who had been offered a place at a local college. She was going to go out on day-release and do a fashion course. Unfortunately, there were some complications with authorities and she wasn't allowed out. We saw her work and she was so talented. Apparently, her response had been: 'Fine. I'll go when I get out.'

There was a funny moment when we walked on to one wing. All the women were sitting at the top of the stairs chatting and it went very quiet when they saw us – it was really awkward. In the end, Alicya (the brave one, remember!) went up the stairs, closely followed by Mandana and myself. She tried to break the ice but they weren't really talking, so she whipped out a packet of cigarettes and this seemed to help the conversation along. We couldn't see any ashtrays around and one of the girls told Mandana to put her fag out on the floor. When we went back downstairs, the deputy governor (who'd been watching the whole time) told us that smoking on the landing was a nickable offence and we could all get an extra three days inside for it! It was only then that we realised none of the inmates had lit their fags – they were trying to get us into trouble!

The Deputy Governor took us to an adjudication room. That was scary. It had a huge table with one chair at one end and three at the other. He explained that the Governor sits on one side and the prisoner (with a P.O. either side of her) sits on the other. It was like a courtroom with no jury. He showed us the list of punishments for offences inside that ranged from loss of spends to days in solitary and additional days on sentences.

He asked us if we fancied seeing what it was like to be locked in a real solitary cell. We all said yes but we went in together, which I was very glad about. The walls were painted white; there was a cardboard bedpan that looked like a fancy-dress cowboy hat and a sponge mattress on the floor. When he locked the door we stopped talking for a while and walked around (as much as possible in such a tiny space). It was weird. There were a few burn marks on the windowsill and lots of graffiti on the walls. Mandana found a really long, very beautiful poem written which made us all a bit weepy. When we were let out, about two minutes later, it felt as if we'd been in there for weeks. We were all quiet and subdued and a bit depressed.

As we left the prison, there was another very sad moment that will always stay in my mind. We were walking along the covered walkway when we heard some shouting. I looked up and I could see two faces at a tiny window a few floors up. They were shouting 'goodbye' and 'thanks for coming' and 'come and visit again soon'. That really drove home the fact that we were going back to our lives and they weren't. We talked amongst ourselves on the way home about how guilty we felt about leaving and how immense it is to take away someone's freedom.

The Consultant – Women In Prison

Before dedicating her life to women prisoners' rights, Chris Tchaikovsky's profession was fraud. In a ten-year criminal career, which began in the 1960s with breaking and entering, she forged post-office books and Eurocheques. She would travel across the country and around the Continent, cashing fraudulent cheques, withdrawing money under false pretences and living it up on the proceeds. By her own admission, she was a 'very successful criminal in terms of material gain', and 'enjoyed the crime and the criminals.'

Tchaikovsky saw the majority of the two-and-a-quarter years she served at Her Majesty's Pleasure as payback: 'If you can't do the time, don't do the crime,' she used to think. 'I had always seen prison as an occupational hazard, a place where you saw your mates and did your time. Then, when a woman burnt to death in her cell, it all changed.'

It was this tragic event that changed Tchaikovsky's mind about prison for ever, and eventually led her to set up 'Women In Prison'. Today, this organisation campaigns for the rights of incarcerated women and supports ex-prisoners on their release. With an encyclopaedic knowledge of what really goes on in women's prisons, what kind of women are jailed and how they cope inside, Tchaikovsky is ideally qualified to be a technical adviser on *Bad Girls*. She is now based in a leafy area of north London, not far from HMP Holloway, but although she is still geographically close, prison is no longer an occupational hazard for Tchaikovsky. She does, however, still regularly visit other inmates, and sits on some of the prison's committees and advisory groups.

It was the death of inmate Patricia Cumming that changed Tchaikovsky's attitude towards the prison system. She recalls: 'Being sent down for two years at the Old Bailey was a wake-up call in itself, but I had got bored of crime and wanted to leave it behind anyway and go to university. Then this woman on the observation corridor set fire to herself. She died because the alarm system which was in place was sabotaged by the officers so as not to go off; they couldn't be bothered dealing with the hassle. When they got to her, it was too late.'

If that wasn't shocking enough, within 24 hours Cumming's cell was repainted and her card removed from outside: 'It was as if she never existed.' Tchaikovsky confesses: 'That got to me. I hadn't thought about anyone dying in there and I hadn't thought what would happen if they did. So, when I heard that 'men from the Home Office' (who were actually coroners) were coming, I knew I had to let them know what had happened. They came and I started walking towards them, and I was literally jumped on by three or four officers. Because I was surprised, like a dope I fought back, so I looked exactly like the crazy person they were protecting the coroners from. I did manage to shout that the alarm had been sabotaged – "The bell was bent back. Check the bell!" – before I was bundled off.'

Later, another inmate miscarried her baby into a bucket and almost bled to death. Along with others on her Wing, Tchaikovsky formed the 'Prisoners' Action Group' and asked for simple, basic human rights, such as officers answering emergency bells, and the right to exercise. 'Petitions were signed but someone was told they wouldn't get their parole and everyone started backtracking and saying they had been coerced into signing. We were divided and ruled and we were threatened with the charge of incitement to mutiny. We thought bugger that, so we barricaded ourselves in my cell. I couldn't care less about anything.'

The charges were eventually reduced to 'offending against good order and discipline' and Tchaikovsky was sentenced to seven days down the solitary block. Mysteriously, within three days, a couple of officers came to tell Tchaikovsky she was free to go. 'They told me that my parole, which had been turned down with no chance of review, had been granted and I was free to go. I couldn't believe it. I knew what was happening though: they wanted me out because they thought I was a troublemaker.'

In a sense, they were right. After she completed her philosophy degree, Tchaikovsky had some involvement with other prison-reform organisations and was considering a career in politics. Then she met another ex-prisoner in the street: 'She told me the new Holloway was worse than the old, that the women were banged up twenty-three-and-a-half hours a day and that another woman had burnt to death.'

Stunned, Tchaikovsky visited a friend still in Holloway and found that everything the woman had said was true. She then approached someone on the Greater London Authority's Women's Committee and wrote to the coroner, mentioning Patricia Cumming's earlier death. 'I realised that these women were invisible and that someone needed to campaign for them.'

Today, Women In Prison deals with two thousand prisoners a year. Homes are found for them on release, they see family law solicitors, receive bursaries for training courses, and a dedicated youth resettlement worker helps the younger women. 'We give private spends to women who have no one on the outside. What that means is they can have new underwear instead of second-hand. If they've got children and they get a temporary release to see them for an afternoon, it means they can buy them a McDonald's. It helps us get clothes for women, radios for those who haven't got them. Imagine being locked up for twenty-three hours a day without a radio for company.'

As well as offering practical help, the organisation campaigns vociferously on issues that otherwise may go unaddressed: 'Issues like the strip-searching by prison officers of women, up to forty per cent of whom have been sexually abused in childhood,' Tchaikovsky explains. 'Then there's Crown Immunity. The Crown cannot prosecute the Crown which means that rats and cockroaches can run rampant and environmental health officers have no jurisdiction. It means if staff are short in any prison, you are given your lunch to eat in your cell next to a lavatory. 'Then there's the transportation of prisoners: shunted into trucks like cattle, where they often feel sick, often need the toilet, with no facilities or even seatbelts.' The list is depressingly long.

As an adviser on *Bad Girls*, Tchaikovsky is obviously invaluable: 'I had been approached many times before by TV companies, who saw the dramatic possibilities of a women's prison but I was never convinced they were genuine in their concern for prisoners themselves. Then Maureen Chadwick, whom I had known for some time, and Ann McManus came along and it was quite clear they wanted to make a difference. They wanted to highlight the issues surrounding women in prison as well as producing a quality drama.'

Tchaikovsky therefore agreed to be an adviser, not simply acting as a sounding board on the details of prison life, but also suggesting storylines herself.

Tchaikovsky says *Bad Girls* hits the right balance in its representation of prisoners and officers: 'They don't do the stereotyping in *Bad Girls*. Before, women prisoners were either deeply unattractive, weak and inadequate or had mental health problems. *Bad Girls* shows there are some very attractive women in prison: very loud, humorous and aggressive and feisty. There are also the terribly damaged, but to always project the one side of the coin is inaccurate. Similarly, there are good officers: kind, caring and determined to help the women. But there is always a Bodybag,' she smiles. 'If the writers hadn't achieved that balance, it could have been disastrous. If it was biased against prison officers, all it would be doing is playing into the hands of the senior civil servants who blame the officers for everything.'

While disparaging of certain documentaries about prison – 'They have murdered the truth', Tchaikovsky argues that drama such as *Bad Girls* tells the truth. 'It annoys me when people question the series' authenticity. The stories are true. Everything that happens in *Bad Girls* has happened or could happen: we know that.' There will be prisoners, ex-prisoners and families of prisoners who will recognise something. The essence of every programme is truthful.'

Through her work, Tchaikovsky knows that prisoners, prison officers, governors and senior civil servants all watch *Bad Girls*; most enjoy it. 'There are some who are hostile towards it but that's because it is truthful. They are all aware of what goes on inside, I think it's a shock for them to see it on television.'

Tchaikovsky has high hopes for *Bad Girls*. She sees it as a campaigning lever that expands the definition of women prisoners beyond the old stereotypes and encourages the audience to think about what kind of women are in prison and why. 'I see the move to popularise the women and present the issues as a fantastic combination. 'What it does is make women who are invisible, who are locked away and not talked about, visible again. *Bad Girls* brings them into people's living rooms, raising issues in a humane, empathetic way. It's quite subversive,' she says. 'And one more thing, I hope the Queen watches it. Prisons do carry her name, after all.' Chris Tchaikovsky laughs. Quite an inspiration.

The Actors Speak – Cast Interviews

INTRODUCTION

It is the *Bad Girls* actors we have to thank for bringing such an extraordinary range of strong characters to life. From the outset, the core cast took time to visit prisons and talk to inmates and staff to help understand the world and people they were portraying. They observed the strange mix of tragedy, adversity, bravery and humour found in women's prisons and brought it all to life in Larkhall's G-Wing.

Some *Bad Girls* actors, such as Helen Fraser and Jack Ellis, had already enjoyed great success in theatre and TV. But for many others – a lot of them young women – this was their first TV role. All are now recognisable faces. They have had to come to terms with the sackfuls of mail, being stopped in the street by admiring fans and the constant attention of the press.

The actors not only work hard together – they play hard together too. The camaraderie and genuine warmth and affection between cast members is easily seen on screen and makes Larkhall a place nine million viewers want to

Simone Lahbib

The first thing you notice when Simone Lahbib enters a room – apart from, of course, her broad smile, luscious lips and twinkling eyes – is her hair. Lustrous and full-bodied, it could almost be from a shampoo advert; like she just stepped out of a salon, in fact. She laughs at this suggestion: 'Oh aye, I use one of those shampoos for fine and flyaway hair.' Lahbib laughs again; she has a very dirty laugh.

Lahbib has a lot to laugh about, as she plays the character of Helen Stewart, who has captured *Bad Girls* fans' hearts and minds. Her portrayal of the graduate, governor grade, fast tracker is mesmerising. Helen's combination of fierce idealism, uncertain emotions and a sense of justice, tempered by a streak of naivety, make her one of the show's most popular characters. It is a popularity for which Lahbib is thankful. 'I get letters telling me that I am a role model and I really get a kick out of that,' she admits. 'I've had so many letters saying I've inspired people to stand up to their boss or quit their job or whatever and that is such a good feeling. To feel like I am making a difference to people's lives.'

Lahbib's praise of *Bad Girls* fans is heartfelt: 'On the whole, they are amazing. They turn up wherever we go, show support whatever we are doing. After the National TV Awards, my agent was inundated with bouquets of flowers and lovely presents. To feel all that love was breathtaking.'

Helen's popularity with the fans has rubbed off on to Lahbib, whose star has risen dramatically since taking on the role. Before *Bad*

'I've had so many letters saying I've inspired people to stand up to their boss or quit their job'

Girls, she had appeared in a number of series, the most notable being *Thief Takers* and *A Young Person's Guide to Becoming A Rock Star*. Lahbib also has a distinguished theatrical background and has starred in a couple of short films. The most recent of these films, *Long Haul*, was recently screened at the Edinburgh International Film Festival, to critical and popular acclaim (not to mention to a host of *Bad Girls* fans!)

With the huge success and prominence of the *Bad Girls* series, Lahbib has been truly taken to heart by the Scottish newspapers, which are famously patriotic. 'In stories about me, I get all the "S" words now: "Stunning Scots actress Simone Lahbib",' she quotes. 'Or "Sensational, sultry, stunning Scot Simone". I suppose I should be grateful they haven't opted for "Slapper Simone"!' She laughs her dirty laugh again.

Lahbib is giddier than her screen persona, but says she still likes Helen a lot, even if she does have her flaws. 'She's very caring, very warm and quite a passionate person. I think she's been very brave since her life has been turned inside out by falling in love with Nikki,' she muses. 'Helen is by no means perfect; she makes mistakes and she can be overly idealistic, although that's one of the things I like about her.'

Importantly, Helen's dress sense has also got a lot better. 'I think we all saw Series One and thought: "She doesn't suit those clothes, does she? Those twinsets have got to go!"' Lahbib chuckles. 'I'm quite glad about that. And actually, that fits with Helen's journey. She's out of a relationship in which she wasn't entirely happy and has fallen in love with someone else. It's true that when you meet someone, you take care of your appearance a bit more. She's got a bit funkier and has had her hair done...'

Lahbib herself is taking the higher public profile in her stride. She confesses to being a private person but not shy, explaining: 'Sometimes I am "on" and other times I am "off".' When she is off duty, as it were, there's nothing Lahbib likes better than getting a massage, throwing a dinner party ('I do a very good roast lamb dinner') or spending quality time with her fiancé, who is also an actor. She returns to Scotland as often as she can.

Born in Stirling to a Scottish mother and a French-Algerian father, Lahbib says she had a 'magic childhood', despite some unfortunate instances of racist bullying. 'Stirling is a great place to grow up. When you still enjoy going out on your bike, it's great – countryside in every direction. I had a wonderful time there, my family still lives in the area. I lived in Edinburgh for a number of years and have lots of friends there, and it's great going back.'

It was in Scotland that Lahbib went to drama school and did most of her theatrical work. 'I spent four years at ballet school, too,' she recalls. 'But I never thought it was a path for me. And if you saw me at ballet school, you'd say the same.' This time, her laugh is tinged with typical Scottish self-deprecation. 'I had a fantastic time at drama school and then did lots of theatre; I played Cathy in *Wuthering Heights* and that was just amazing to do.'

From the passion with which she talks about it, theatre is obviously close to Lahbib's heart. She says she enjoys the rehearsal process: 'You can play, explore, take risks'. She also loves the experience of performing live in front of an audience every night: 'That's the time you become better as an actor. In television, you don't get rehearsals or read-throughs, so you have to make instant decisions. You play, not necessarily safe, but you'll do what you know works rather than take risks.' Which isn't to say Lahbib doesn't enjoy television, or indeed film. 'I love the constant taking on of new things in TV; you're always moving, you never get a chance to get bored.'

'This place is a madhouse but I do love it'

Lahbib would like film to feature more in her future, possibly directing, but she is very happy with her lot at the moment. 'I'm not worried Helen will overshadow anything else I might do. Once you do something else, you become associated with that, so we'll see what happens.'

The camaraderie and good humour that is apparent on the *Bad Girls* set must go some way towards nurturing Lahbib's contentment. She confirms that it is a fun place to work at. 'One of the funniest things was the day we had an extra in with no knickers. She was up on the first floor and stood with her legs well apart. One by one, the crew and then all of us walked underneath and had a look!' She laughs heartily once more. 'This place is a madhouse but I do love it. I like an adventure.'

Mandana Jones

Mandana Jones has a secret criminal past which saw her pursued by the police, then imprisoned and finally forced to confess her crime. 'Well, I did actually do it,' she grins. 'For weeks I denied it, but in the end I came clean and admitted it was a fair cop.'

The dirty deed was theft – of a cheekbone highlighter pencil from Boots. It cost 69p. Jones was fifteen. 'I had got a Boots' voucher for Christmas from an auntie and I was in the shop and I saw the highlighter. I thought it wasn't worth breaking up my £5 token for and I thought it would be much more fun to nick it. So that's what I did.' Caught by a store detective, she was shipped off to a police station where Jones still protested her innocence when her father picked her up. 'I only admitted I meant to do it when a policeman came round to the house a few weeks later.'

If nothing else, Jones now doesn't have time to shoplift (nor does she have any need to artificially highlight her elegant cheekbones). When she's not playing Nikki Wade, Jones is busy answering fan mail, living what she calls 'a rock-and-roll' lifestyle, watching her new giant TV or, as an avid yoga devotee, meditating.

She says playing Nikki has been fantastic for her, not just because Nikki is a great character: 'I love how she is incredibly outspoken, honest and intelligent and not scared. Playing someone as confident as she is, I think it would be great to be like that. Sometimes, it's hard to achieve because I'm not like that, but in the last few years my self-confidence has certainly grown and I think that's to do with playing Nikki. And,' she smirks, 'I love her trowel action.'

Jones, whose mother is Iranian and her father Welsh, says the success of the show makes her incredibly proud, especially after the drubbing it received at the hands of the critics. 'That all the grown-up newspapers slated it and the public liked it and it won awards was a magic feeling. Normally, when you're in something and it gets a pounding, it means the end is near but, with *Bad Girls*, it goes from strength to strength.'

But *Bad Girls* also gives Jones a more personal sense of achievement. 'I have had some astonishing letters that say things like "My life is easier because of you" and "My parents, who threw me out the house when I told them I was

'With *Bad Girls*, it goes from strength to strength'

gay, have asked me to come home again after eighteen months." It's very exciting to think that you're doing something like that, something that is causing some sort of positive change. Everybody wants to make a difference in life and I feel very privileged to have been given the opportunity to do so.'

It would be hard to imagine Jones as anyone other than Nikki but, originally, she was in line for the role of Helen. 'I turned up at the audition and Brian Park said: 'How do you feel about the lesbian lifer?' I was like "Sure" and, after I read it, I instinctively really liked her and thought she was much more interesting to play and very different from my previous role.' Before *Bad Girls*, Jones played Dr Sam Haynes in the soap *London Bridge*. 'There were only three things I could do,' she chuckles: 'I could test your reflexes. I had a little torch which I looked into people's eyes or ears with, usually if they had started having dizzy spells as a precursor to a brain tumour. And towards the end, I got to do a bit of blood-pressure taking.'

And she was also bound, gagged, tied to a chair and threatened with Methadone-laced coffee for two days. 'I was being held hostage by my psychotic receptionist,' Jones explains matter-of-factly. Sounds like Larkhall was a lucky escape. Wasn't she wary of playing a lesbian character, though?

'I don't want to be labelled "the lesbian one" but when I say that, I mean it in the same way as when a drama introduces a black family or a

gay couple – in inverted commas. Ultimately, it's patronising and it's shite and means that the characters don't have characteristics beyond the fact that they're black or they're gay.

'My opinion is that if you're not going to do it properly, there's no point in doing it at all. I didn't want to be the stereotypical, typecast lesbian because, completely selfishly, I don't think it would do my career any good, but also because it would be uninteresting and a disservice. I do get letters which say it's good not to see a stereotype.'

For someone who is clearly an emotive, enthralling actress, Jones fell into the profession almost by accident. 'It was around that time everyone is in a frenzy about going to university and all I knew was that I didn't want to read any more books or write any more essays. I obviously

looked troubled because the Head of English came up to me and asked if I was all right. I explained that everyone else seemed to know what they were going to do with the next forty years of their lives and I hadn't a clue. She suggested I do acting because she thought I was good at it. She may as well have said I should go to the moon.'

Instead of going to the moon, Jones set about building her CV. The first brick: a job in London's West End. 'I worked as an usherette, selling Toblerone and souvenir programmes, at the Piccadilly Theatre where *Mutiny* was on with David Essex and Sinitta. There was this one rock number that David Essex sang that went: "Hell! I live in Hell! Hell, Hell burns free!" I had to listen to that eight times a week,' Jones says, faux stony-faced. 'I remember once I was up in the gods and I started crying because I had had enough of hearing that song.'

Luckily, then, she got into drama school and the rest was far from hellish. Happy in her work, Jones is now managing her personal life. 'There are two me's: the rock-and-roll me who enjoys going out, drinking, smoking and having a rip-roaring time; and there's the yoga me who goes away to retreats at Christmas – it's much more fun than getting vaguely pissed and vaguely bored and watching telly – and gets excited about herbal tea. I think

'I didn't want to be the stereotypical, typecast lesbian'

I need to become the yoga me all the time but I'll miss the rock-and-roll me if I do.'

Jones is only too aware how lucky she has been to play Nikki. 'I'm bloody lucky,' she says. 'It's a fantastic job – a popular character in a popular show – and it's fun to do. It's really and truly a super job in the profession.'

Jack Ellis

Jack Ellis was shocked when he read about a real life Jim Fenner. 'This officer was married to one of the senior wardens, having an affair with another warden and having another affair with a prisoner too. He would take the prisoner out to the local pub, have sex with her in the car and then take her back to prison. He got done and his only punishment was to get moved to another prison, something he was keen on anyway.' He shakes his head in slightly amused disbelief.

You can understand Ellis' disbelief. Perhaps more than any other character, Fenner has revealed truths of prison life that have shocked many. 'He is an unreconstructed male who can be harsh in a lot of situations. He is sexually motivated and has dubious morals. For example, he doesn't think it's wrong to hit a woman. At the same time, he can be quite fair. He can deal with situations and thinks on his feet. When he saved Karen from Tessa Spall, that was him thinking quickly and saving Karen's life. I think he is a good prison officer and he gets respect from the women, even though he is a bit rotten. From doing research in both men's and women's prisons, I know there are officers like Jim Fenner out there. Not many, but they are there.'

With Fenner presenting such a complex character, in the beginning Ellis was unsure how to play him. 'It was exciting but nerve-wracking. The first half of Series One was fantastic for me

'I know there are officers like Jim Fenner out there'

because I was working out how nasty – and how nice – he could be. I loved the storylines surrounding Shell, Rachel Hicks and him. It was a real meaty challenge for me to get my teeth into.'

Since then, Ellis has also enjoyed Fenner's relationship with Yvonne, whom he describes as a fantastic character. 'The way Yvonne and Jim spark off each other is great, the struggle for

power that goes on between them is fascinating and fun to play.'

Despite being one of the original cast members, Ellis hadn't got to grips with how successful *Bad Girls* was until lately. 'It's a bit like being inside a bubble,' he explains. 'The popularity of the show only really started dawning on me the morning after we had won the *TV Quick* award. Before then, I knew it was good but afterwards I realised how popular it was. And when I found out about the fans on the internet, I was amazed.'

The reaction from the public also persuaded him that *Bad Girls* had quite a following: 'It's always a nice reaction, I get: "Oi, Fenner," that kind of thing; there's never been any abuse. A lot of people say: "You're a good actor," or "That's a good part you play," so there's no problem with people not differentiating between the actor and the character.' Lucky for Ellis.

But what would he do if he saw Fenner in the street? 'Oh, I'd watch him,' he says enthusiastically. 'He's so devious, he's fascinating. He'd probably make me like him and then gradually I'd discover his true nature. He is a great character to play.'

Until he was thirteen, Ellis fostered ambitions to be a fireman and a farmer. Then he saw his eldest brother Robin, who would later rise to fame in the TV series *Poldark*, starring in *The Importance of Being Earnest*. 'From then on, I was hooked. The excitement and the anticipation were so intoxicating. I knew acting was what I wanted to do and eventually I went to drama school.'

Since graduating, Ellis has become a well-known face on British TV. He starred three times in *Prime Suspect* with Helen Mirren, as D.I. Muddiman, and in one series of the customs and excise drama, *The Knock*. 'That was pretty tough. I played Eddie Barton, a customs officer who had motor neurone disease. As the series progressed, his condition deteriorated and he threw himself under a tube train.'

Ellis has also played a psychopath in *City Central* and has been in 'the standards like *The Bill* and *Casualty*'. He is also an excellent stage actor with an exemplary theatrical pedigree. He has worked at the Royal Shakespeare Company, with feted director Mark Rylance and, in the late 1970s, he founded the Actors' Touring Company which is still going strong today. 'I have played Horatio in *Hamlet* and Don Pedro in *Much Ado About Nothing*, both directed by Mark Rylance. We even took *Hamlet* into Broadmoor, where we performed in front of Peter Sutcliffe, the Yorkshire Ripper, and Dennis Nilsen.'

Quite an experience for anyone; it also helped

equip Ellis when it came to understanding prisons and prison officers. 'There is a sense of incarceration, a smell of captivity that is really hard to describe,' he recalls. 'I went to visit a men's prison in advance of playing Fenner, and watching the wardens was just fascinating. They have a real energy, an adrenaline running through them the whole time. They're watching, counting, wondering if anything's going to happen. There's a real tension there.'

Happily married with two children, Ellis couldn't be more different from Fenner: 'I'm a middle-class boy who went to public school, so in a way it's odd I play the roles that I do. I think it's the way I look,' he says. He also confesses to enjoying cooking, playing cricket and watching football. He is also a real current-affairs

'We even took *Hamlet* into Broadmoor, where we performed in front of Peter Sutcliffe, the Yorkshire Ripper'

aficionado. '*Question Time*, *Panorama*, *Newsnight*: I don't miss them. I love the news too.'

Perhaps unusually, Ellis isn't so keen on watching TV dramas, saying it has to be very good to keep his attention. He has a soft spot for comedy, from *Morecambe and Wise* to *Smack the Pony*. 'I love Steve Coogan and very much admire Harry Enfield too. Comedy is becoming more surreal and that's much more to my taste.'

More than anything, starring in *Bad Girls* has taught Ellis that situations aren't always black and white. 'I have realised how much greyer things are and how the whole punitive system needs to be sorted out. I'm a liberal at heart and reform is badly needed. A kid of eighteen goes into prison, for example, and they'll come out a heroin addict. Plus, because women's prisons are few and far between, when women are sentenced, they are often sent to prisons miles away from home. Many are mothers who have dependent families to care for. It's just not right.' How thankfully unlike Fenner Jack Ellis is.

Debra Stephenson

When Debra Stephenson first 'met' Shell Dockley, some two-and-a-half years ago, she was uncompromising in her assessment: 'Don't feel sorry for her,' she said at the time. 'A psychopathic, jealous woman; she set fire to a woman who was seeing her boyfriend. The judge at her trial called her "evil personified" and I agree with him.'

Nearly three years of living with Shell, who has been dubbed 'a deranged Alexis Colby for the millennium', Stephenson is more circumspect: 'I think on the first series, there was only one level to her but I really wanted to find other levels to her. With the second series, I got that chance. I think she still is a bitch and a bully but we now know why she is and that extra dimension helps you sympathise with her. But then, just as you think she's not that bad and she's had a tough time, she does something really despicable. That keeps her interesting because you don't lose the ambiguities and the complexities of her character.'

It is testimony to the complexities of the writing of Shell's character and the nuances of Stephenson's acting that she garnered a most popular actress nomination at last year's National TV Awards. 'I felt I was representing the show,' she says candidly. 'Shell is a strong character just because she is so bad and such a bitch. I think that makes her the epitome of a bad girl.'

It's all such a long way from the tense months that were spent making the first series and then waiting to see what the audience's reaction would be. Stephenson recalls those days with a fondness almost akin to the wartime Blitz spirit: 'It's really difficult to tell when you're so involved with something whether it's going to work or not. I don't think Brian [Park] really knew whether it would be a success. I think he was confident and we all felt it was good but we didn't know if the public would take to it.'

Despite the praise and accolades, playing Shell hasn't radically altered Stephenson as a person, and hasn't changed her life in general. 'I get recognised but that's about all really,' she

'Just as you think she's not that bad and she's had a tough time, she does something really despicable'

says with a shrug. 'I'm still me, no matter what.'

Before *Bad Girls*, Stephenson was best known for playing ditzy blonde Diane in *Playing the Field*. 'As a blonde, those are the parts you get,' she explains. 'As well as two series of *Playing the Field*, I did a sitcom for kids in which I played a dippy hippy; I seem to be good at the dippy hippy stuff. That's why playing someone like Shell is so good – it's a complete departure from what people expect of me.'

Stephenson is originally from Hull, where her desire to perform bloomed. 'In Hull, there wasn't a great deal going on, particularly so for a fourteen-year-old, I was just doing talent competitions and playing in working men's clubs. It was a bit like *Little Voice*: I used to do singing impressions and impersonations. Then,

I did *Opportunity Knocks'.*

Determined to break into showbusiness, Stephenson saw this route as the only one open to her at the time. Though she didn't win, she made it through to the grand final and it provided her with exposure and a taste for the limelight. It did have its drawbacks however. 'After I did *Opportunity Knocks*, I got a letter from a bloke asking me to send him a pair of my socks. At the time, I didn't really understand the full implications of it but my parents were like: "No, I don't think you should send him socks." It was only years later I found out about sock fetishists and I was like, "Oh my God. I was only fourteen." '

In the years that followed between then and going to drama school, Stephenson did panto, worked as an alternative comedienne in student bars and at the Edinburgh Fringe and did some radio comedy, some of which also featured comedian Alan Davies: 'That was wonderful. That was when I definitely knew I wanted to be an actress no matter what.' Stephenson's first job upon graduating from drama school was in *Reckless* with Robson Green. 'I played Francesca Annis' character's secretary. It was a small part but Paul Abbott, the writer, was so nice, he was rewriting it as they went along so my part got a bit bigger.' Then, after *Playing the Field* and a role in the comedy *People Like Us*, along came *Bad Girls*.

But prison has taken its toll on the now-married Stephenson: 'At the beginning of the run, it was dark when we arrived and it was dark when we left: I didn't see the sunshine all day and that was hard-going.'

So Stephenson is heading for pastures new. With Shell's escape, the actress is bidding farewell to HMP Larkhall. ' I would never say never to coming back but I do have this fear at

the back of my mind that playing Shell will take over my life. Playing other roles has got to be part of my career and I don't want to be remembered as Shell Dockley forever.'

With that in mind, Stephenson has already branched out, starring in a Catherine Cookson drama last year. 'It was nice to do

'I would never say never to coming back'

something completely different: a corset and a high-necked frock, a good girl rather than a bad girl, riding round on horses in the countryside. It was quite a transformation,' she laughs. Stephenson has also returned to her comedy roots and has recorded a pilot sketch show for which 'I had to get a day-release!'

As for the future, Stephenson has no firm plans. 'We'll just wait and see what happens. I will miss the other girls – returning to set after a break is like coming back to school – but it's time for me to move on. I won't ever forget Shell and I think she'll stay close to a lot of people's hearts too.'

Just as long as she isn't armed with a broken bottle...

Helen Fraser

Helen Fraser has imagined a whole life for Sylvia 'Bodybag' Hollamby. 'All she wants to do is finish at 5pm so she can get home – she's quite a home bird – and see her Bobby and make his dinner. I am convinced she shops at Iceland and Sylvia's dream is for her and Bobby to retire to their mobile home in Lee-on-Sea.' And the children? 'Well, Constance, or Connie, has her own family now. Gail, the middle one, is still a cause for concern. Then there's little Bobby-Darren at university and that's costing the Hollambys rather a lot. He's a bit of a handful; I think he was an afterthought.'

From the tone of her voice and her imaginings, it's clear that Fraser regards Sylvia with fondness, despite her often despicable behaviour. 'She does do terrible and vile things but I think she thinks she's doing her job in the best way she can. She's old-fashioned and she'd like to lock them up twenty-four hours a day. She thinks they've done something wrong so they should be punished.'

Nevertheless, Sylvia's recent exploits have shocked even Fraser. 'Before Karen Betts made her part of the riot team to free Jim (with whom she's secretly in love) from Shell, I never knew I could be so fierce. In the helmet, shield, boiler suit and hob-nailed boots, I look like Boadicea! And then getting Shell moved to the psychiatric wing was a horrible thing to do. Recently, I saw a clip of Sylvia and Betty Wheeler walking down the corridor and I said to the director "I'd hate to meet those two on a dark night".'

'Sylvia's dream is for her and Bobby to retire to their mobile home in Lee-on-Sea'

But the Oldham-born Fraser insists her character isn't all bad. 'She shed a tear when Zandra Plackett had her baby and she offered Yvonne a cup of tea when her husband didn't turn up for a visit. There is a hint of humanity there.'

For those who have followed Fraser's long and distinguished career, Sylvia is quite a revelation.

She has had parts in classic films like *Billy Liar* and *Repulsion* and theatre roles in the West End and around the country opposite the likes of Judi Dench in plays by Alan Bennett and Harold Pinter. She also has an impressive comedy repertoire including seven series of *The Dick Emery Show* and appearances in *The Two Ronnies* and *Rising Damp*.

'I did about twelve films and I should say that half of those will always be classics. That's a lovely feeling because they can never be wiped away. *Billy Liar* will be there until I am a very old lady and I have visions of my being interviewed and someone showing a clip. And with *Repulsion*, Roman Polanski was just starting out and I didn't realise how important he was going to be.'

She has similar feelings about her comedy roles: 'Comedians are so insecure and so nervous, they have to get to trust you. A gag is only as good as its feed and I think that's why Dick [Emery] kept me on for so long. He liked to have real actors around him who knew their skill and who could set up the gag. You weren't allowed to get a laugh, I have to say, but I was quite flattered because each comedian I worked with asked me back. I worked with Ronnie Corbett on *Sorry* and he asked me to do *The Two Ronnies*. I thought I must have got something right.' Fraser, however, has never been cast as a baddie, nor ever had such fan mail as she does now. 'It's very flattering,' she says, 'when you get letters that say: "You make us laugh until the tears run down our face."'

It was because of a small part in *Coronation Street*, playing Magenta, a hypnotist who attempted to help Jack give up smoking, that Maureen Chadwick thought Fraser ideal to play Sylvia. Fraser says she never imagined *Bad Girls* would be such a success but she also knew immediately that she was right for the part of Sylvia.

'I've always played the maid, never an above-stairs part, and suddenly I realised I was too old for the maid and I was on to playing the housekeeper. I thought it was time to change the image I had previously – of the plump next-door neighbour who never got the boy – and move on. Sylvia was such a good part and I thought: "In for a penny, in for a pound", and that's why I look like the back end of a bus. I wear the most unflattering uniforms and no make-up except a bit of mascara, which I wear for my sanity. It's very hard when you're sitting there in the make-up room and the others are having their blue eye shadow put on and their hair done and I arrive and they take off what I've put on and scrub my face.'

For as long as she can remember, Fraser has wanted to be an actress. She went to a theatrical boarding school when she was nine where 'the education was appalling but I learned other things'. She elaborates: 'Come the one o'clock lunch bell, it's into ballet shoes or tap shoes, which is wonderful as a child but it means acting is the only thing I can do. I may not have learnt

'It's very flattering when you get letters that say: "You make us laugh until the tears run down our face"'

lots of maths but people say to me I never look nervous and that's because we were taught how to present ourselves. I'm quaking like everyone else, I just don't show it.'

In between series of *Bad Girls*, Fraser, who lives in 'deepest Suffolk', has returned to the stage in a one-woman show she wrote herself about Vespa Victoria, the music-hall entertainer. It was greeted with rave reviews. Fraser admits a love of theatre, though her husband, sound recordist Peter Handford who won an Oscar for his work on *Out of Africa*, can't understand her fascination. 'I have to explain to him that if you do a film, you get it right after five or ten takes, but in the theatre, if you miss a laugh on a Tuesday night, you're determined to get it on a Wednesday. To handle an audience, to get an audience to laugh with you, it was what I was trained for.'

And captivate an audience she does, never more so than as Sylvia. 'She's the comic relief and they give me a lot of fantastic one-liners which, for a comedy actress, is a joy. And long may that continue.' So she doesn't see Sylvia's retirement to Lee-on-Sea looming on the horizon? 'There are so many things that Sylvia wants because she loves her home and, although she'd very much like to retire with her Bobby, I think she thinks if she did just another year, she could pay for more things. Besides, I think Larkhall might collapse if Sylvia left.'

Claire King

Claire King has cheekbones you could cut yourself on. With her mane of blonde hair and a suggestive look in her eye, there is something playful and almost feline about the actress formerly known as *Emmerdale*'s Kim Tate.

Now recognised as Karen Betts, King considers her new character trustworthy, solid and a bit lonely. And much nicer than her previous incarnation. 'Kim was a brilliant character to

'She has exceedingly dodgy taste in men'

play: you could be over-the-top and camp and she was an out-and-out bitch. She did have a soft side but it didn't appear that often. Karen, on the other hand, you'd trust as a mate. She is firm but fair and she treats people properly. I think you can see that in the way she has treated Shell and Sylvia in the past.'

King believes Karen also has a wild streak which she keeps hidden at work. 'I think she's a different person away from that job, I think you'd have to be. It must be hard not taking the job home with you, particularly if you're Wing Governor.' She may admire Karen's professionalism but there's something of which King is not so sure: 'She has exceedingly dodgy taste in men. I think it's a case of falling for the wrong guy. I think she has a real blind spot as far as Jim Fenner is concerned and she really can't see the evil side of him. She's still a single woman. I reckon she's fairly lonely and her job means she's got to be fairly disciplined and on the ball, so I can't imagine her having a mad social life. And the choice of men at the prison is a bit limited. Josh is a bit too young for her, I suppose. Though he might make a good toy boy...' King is playful indeed.

It was this quality, amongst others, that persuaded Brian Park to cast King as Karen. King jumped at the chance of appearing in *Bad Girls*: 'I'd seen the first series and thought it was great, so when Brian asked me if I wanted to do it, I felt very lucky.'

It had been over a year since King had left *Emmerdale* after a nine-year stint, and she was eager to work again, having taken some time off to relax and 'have a real life'.

'I live in North Yorkshire and have dogs and horses to look after and, when I left *Emmerdale* the first time, it was great spending time at

home with the animals. After I left that time, they rang up two weeks later and asked me to come back. I was like, "Hang on. I'm dead and I haven't had time to get used to unemployment." They offered me a new deal and I went back and it was a case of mistaken identity and it wasn't Kim who had died at all. I ended up staying for about a year and a half but then I wanted to move on.'

Move on she did, even though it was a tough decision to make: 'Leaving a soap is a risk because there has been a snotty attitude towards actors who have been in soaps. I think that's changing now but I don't blame anyone for staying in a soap for years and years. It's a decent living, you're working hard, you're at home, your family is round you and it's a good life. But I felt I had some other stuff in me, I felt like I had to play more than just one character.'

Therefore, after King's sabbatical, Karen replaced Helen Stewart as G-Wing's governor. This necessitated King living in London during the week whilst filming, and travelling home to outside Harrogate at the weekends to see husband Peter Amory, who plays Chris Tate in Emmerdale. King thinks that striking a balance between work and home is essential: 'At the end of the day, life isn't about making TV and entertaining people – though that's great – it's about your loved ones. Your nearest and dearest are the most important things. That's why I make sure I get back every weekend, even if it's just for a day. With Peter being in the business, he understands what it's like when schedules change, but the dogs don't. They just wonder where their mum is.'

King hadn't always planned to be an actress, although her father used to be an actor and that had some impression on her as a child. 'I knew I didn't want a nine-to-five job, I knew I couldn't hack a sensible job so it had to be something to do with entertainment, whether behind or in front of the camera. Music was a big part of my life and that took priority in my teenage years

and early twenties. I was in a band, went drinking with Lemmy from Motorhead and went to nightclubs and parties all the time. After that, I went to drama college and *Emmerdale* came along when I was twenty-six.'

After being a punk rocker and a rock chick, it was, King says, good to settle back into country life. It is this country life to which King attributes her healthy glow. 'Well it can't be anything else,' she chuckles. 'I'm allergic to gyms so the only exercise I get is taking the dogs for a walk or riding. I eat like a pig, drink like a fish and smoke like a chimney. It must be the country air.'

King says she also enjoys the glamour of

It perhaps isn't a surprise that King once planned to be a stunt woman

playing Karen: 'The wardrobe mistress and I agree that Versace and Jean Paul Gaultier suits look better on screen and last longer than anything cheaper. I leave the nylon culottes to the others. The budget's got to go somewhere, after all.'

After being threatened with an infected needle by Tessa Spall, hosed down by Jim Fenner and entrusted with putting a drugged-up Sylvia Hollamby into a taxi, it perhaps isn't a surprise that King once planned to be a stunt woman. 'I was going to do it before *Emmerdale* and I got three disciplines but then Kim Tate came along. I was into all that then. I wouldn't do it now – I'm far too old. Now, it's a major trauma if I break a nail!'

Alicya Eyo

After a hard day at work, playing the part of Denny Blood, there's nothing Alicya Eyo likes better than going home and doing a bit of colouring in. 'It's very relaxing,' she insists. 'I sit with my felt tips and colour, and all the day's stresses evaporate. I think it verges on the therapeutic.'

Yet, sitting down and colouring in is the last thing you might expect Eyo to do, especially as she brings fierceness, volatility and, sometimes, naked aggression to her character in *Bad Girls*. Eyo confirms that she is quite different from her character, Denny. Quiet, unassuming and a bit of an enigma, she says she would consider crossing the road to avoid Denny if she saw her in the street.

Eyo is, however, extremely earnest about the empathy that she feels with the institutionalised character who has touched so many hearts. She comments, in her surprisingly softly spoken voice: 'If it was the Denny of the beginning of the first series, I'd definitely find her scary. Then, she was a real bully; vicious and selfish. Latterly, and in the second series particularly, she has grown up a lot and has more awareness of people round her and their feelings. I think that had a lot to do with meeting her mum and the influence that Yvonne has had over her.' The issues that Eyo has so emphatically played out as Denny have obviously had their effect.

What have been the high points for Eyo of appearing in *Bad Girls*? Eyo has found it brilliant working closely with Denise Black, who played Jessie, and Linda Henry, who plays Yvonne. 'I think my favourite scene of Denny's was when Jessie came to visit her and she told her not to come back until she was sober for a year. That was really moving. And working with Linda is a

> **'I think both prisoners and officers admit that the show is true to life'**

privilege and an education for a young actress like me.'

Eyo notes that the appearance of Shaz has also given Denny an opportunity to have some fun, something Denny missed out on when she was growing up. 'Since she was young, she has spent her entire life within institutions or in foster homes, where she endured both physical and sexual abuse. In prison, she dished it out rather than taking it and I think that was a defence mechanism. With Shaz's appearance, she feels alive for the first time for ages and is catching up on her missed childhood.'

As with the rest of the cast, researching Denny took Eyo to Winchester prison, where she encountered an inmate very similar to Denny. It was an experience that made a lasting impression on her. 'She was a bit older, but she had been in institutions for most of her life and seeing her was very useful in helping me understand what makes someone react in the way Denny does.'

Winchester prison and a later visit to Bullwood Hall gave Eyo an invaluable insight into the world of women's prisons and their representation in *Bad Girls*. 'I think both prisoners and officers admit that the show is true to life, even if we use dramatic licence. What the show does especially well is show the support between the inmates in a women's prison. The strong relationships as well as the loneliness is there. To

Hillsborough playwright Lance Nielson on his new play, *Hi, I'm Vince*, last year, she is determined to make a return to the stage.

Eyo was born and bred in Liverpool, a hint of which is suggested by the lilt in her voice when she gets animated. She says that the biggest inspiration in her life has been her mother, Susan, who sings in a jazz and blues band. 'More than anyone else, she has taught me to pursue my dreams and persevere even if things get tough. She's just started further education, doing what she wants to do. She always makes me feel optimistic for the future and I hope I am strong enough to do what I want to do when I am her age.'

As for the here and now, Eyo wants to continue her film and TV career as well as doing theatre. She has already made a couple of short films and recently made her first feature, *Greenwich Mean Time*. She says she has no ambitions to go to Hollywood and doesn't set herself long-term goals, other than to be happy in whatever she is doing. 'I set myself goals for the year and achieve those. Then, you have a sense of fulfilment and not a feeling of underachievement or not having reached your objectives. That is the only way to live your life as far as I am concerned.'

With two-and-a-half series of *Bad Girls* behind her, Eyo still hasn't become used to the notoriety she has garnered from the public. 'It is weird when

get on in prison, you do have to be a very strong individual and I think that's why Denny copes the way she does – she doesn't see she has any other choice.'

Throughout Eyo's own childhood, the actress originally planned a career as a dancer but fate intervened when the dancing classes she attended every Saturday incorporated drama too. 'It was mainly improvisation and stuff like that. One day when I was around fifteen, I realised I enjoyed it more than I did the dancing and decided then I wanted to be an actress. I still got the moves though,' she says with a wink.

From then on, Eyo progressed rapidly, thanks to good old-fashioned hard

'She was a real bully; vicious and selfish'

work. She has worked regularly in theatre and on television, winning parts in the likes of *Casualty*, *Band of Gold*, *Hetty Wainthropp Investigates* and the legal drama *A Wing and a Prayer*. Theatre still remains close to Eyo's heart, despite her continued success – and demand – on TV. After working with

people come up to me on the street or write nice things about me on the internet. I find it so strange they are talking about me. And going to showbiz parties and events really blows my mind. I mean, I'm just me, aren't I?' Indeed she is – and unique with it.

Joe Shaw

When Joe Shaw first appeared as Dominic McAllister in *Bad Girls*, he couldn't avoid questions about his well-known actor father, Martin. 'You have to accept it because a lot of people are talking to you because of that connection. I started off my first job with him on *Rhodes* [in which he played the young Rhodes to his father's more mature version] and then, when I started doing *Bad Girls*, he was doing a medical series. We used to phone each other up and say stuff like: "What are you doing?" He'd say: "Learning how to put a tube down someone's throat. What are you doing?" and I'd tell him: "I'm learning how to lock a door".

Now, though, Shaw has become a star in his own right. The part of Dominic involved more than merely locking doors, and Shaw relished the role: 'From doing the research and going to Winchester Prison to have a look round there, to working on a brand new series, it was a real experience for me. We were creating something from scratch and that was an amazing thing to do. Plus, Dominic was a great character.'

Indeed he was. All doe eyes and good intentions, he had his share of rude awakenings, tender moments and close calls. Shaw says that, unlike in some other series, developing the character for *Bad Girls* was always important. 'The trouble with a lot of series is that you get thrown right in there and you never get to see a character beyond being a doctor or a policeman or whatever. With Dominic, you saw him being a quiet prison officer and then, slowly, you found out more. He was a bit of a grower.'

'We were creating something from scratch and that was an amazing thing to do'

But after twenty-three episodes, Shaw decided that he had explored Dominic as much as he wanted. 'I always said I was only going to do two series and when the time came, I was confident I was doing the right thing,' he explains. 'One of the nice things about doing *Bad Girls* was that you went in every day and did something different every day. It was quite a

learning curve but, once I learnt, it was time to go and do something else.'

Shaw is looking forward to plenty of new challenges ahead of him. His career, to date, includes roles in *Junk*, the Screen Two film of the award-winning book, and a radio version of *The Chronicles of Narnia*. He also enjoys appearing on stage, and has had a starring role in an Alan Bennett play.

As for the future, Shaw is optimistic: 'I'm young and in a nice position where I've done a little bit of everything, so I am happy whatever happens next, whether it's theatre, film or television.'

Kim Oliver

Chances are that everyone in Keighley, West Yorkshire, already knew Kim Oliver before she made her TV debut as Buki Lester in *Bad Girls*. 'Where I'm from, there weren't many black people,' she reflects, 'and I was always quite outgoing when I was young, so everyone on the bus and in the shops, and wherever else, knew me.'

Oliver's outgoing nature soon translated itself into a desire to perform. She says the film *The Color Purple* had a profound effect on her: 'I thought there were some brilliant female parts in it and it really moved me. I knew when I saw it, acting was what I wanted to do.' And so she

'Strange as it sounds, she's a joy to play'

did. After graduating from drama school in London, it was parts in new plays that really attracted Oliver. It was while she was acting in a recent play that *Bad Girls*' casting director, Margaret Crawford, saw Oliver and offered her the role of Buki.

Oliver admits: 'I have always had an attraction to difficult parts'. 'Difficult' is a word tragically suited to the role of Buki. 'She's the result of the failures of the care system,' Oliver says. 'She has been in care all her life and was abused by a care worker. She self-mutilates because she feels worthless, and wrongly guilty about, and ashamed of, being abused – and she became a prostitute and a crack addict for the same reasons. When I first read the breakdown of Buki's character, I couldn't believe all the terrible things that had befallen her. But having done the research, it's easy to see how these things do happen to young women who are failed by the system. They all link together.'

So good is Oliver, it's surprising that Buki is her first television role. 'My first ever, ever, ever!' she grins. 'Most people have done a couple of episodes of *Casualty* or *The Bill* but this has been my big break. I've been doing it for two months

now and I can still hardly believe I actually got the job. I say to myself: "I got this job! I really got this job!"' Before she joined the show, Oliver went to the pub with her future cellmates, Alicya Eyo and Lindsey Fawcett. 'I got to know them before turning up on set and they were ace. Everyone else has been the same, really lovely and welcoming.'

So, after two months, has the euphoria worn off? 'Not yet,' Oliver grins. 'Buki is a fantastic part to play, It's terrifying because there is so much there and so much going on, so to have time to develop her is a real bonus. And because she's young, she has fun and is cheeky, so there is humour to balance the hard times she has. Strange as it sounds, she's a joy to play.'

Linda Henry

Linda Henry loves playing Yvonne Atkins – and not just because she has the best clothes on the prison block. 'She does, though, doesn't she?' smiles Linda. 'Versace, Gucci, Joseph: I got all of them. I think they must have spent the whole costume budget on my wardrobe – and I get to buy some of it at the end of the series,' she laughs huskily. 'I bought a great Gucci jacket at the end of the last series, the little black leather one and the beautiful lilac suede suit that I wore in my first episode. Of course, I'm too scared to wear either of them now in case something happens to them.'

For some reason, it is hard to imagine Henry being scared of anything. 'Lots of people have said that about me, but it's not true at all. It might be to do with the way I look, it might be because I tend to play strong characters but it has been said over and over, and I actually find it a bit boring. When I do play strong characters, I hope I bring vulnerability to them, and I have played a hell of a lot of victims. In *Trial and Retribution*, I wasn't scary at all, and Sandra Gangel [in *Beautiful Thing*] was a loyal, emotional mother.'

In *Trial and Retribution*, Henry barely spoke at all, but dominated the drama nonetheless as the horrifically mutilated victim of Iain Glen's Nathan. Not surprisingly, it was a role that profoundly affected her: 'Parts I play always affect me but that affected me the most.' Henry worked hard playing the role as accurately as possible. 'My character had had her throat cut so, to get the breathing technique right, I went to the ear, nose and throat hospital and met this wonderful doctor. We worked on the breathing and what people do when they have their throat cut, how they survive it, the trauma they go through, where the breath starts and where it stops. It was fascinating. I don't normally enjoy watching myself on screen – I am awfully self-critical – but I did enjoy watching *Trial and Retribution*. My family couldn't watch it, though, because they found it too harrowing.'

So what was it like joining the *Bad Girls* cast at the end of the first series? 'It was a strong ensemble anyway, so I was very nervous, but

'What I love about Yvonne is that she is incredibly strong and she can be very scary'

with a strong character like Yvonne you have to make the right impression from the word go and that caused me even more worry.' Henry needn't have been nervous, however, since she has an incandescent presence as Yvonne that is mesmerising.

Of her character, Henry says Yvonne is extremely strong but 'she's a puppy inside'. 'What I love about Yvonne is that she is incredibly strong and she can be very scary. She won't let anyone shit on her or anyone she loves, especially her family. But, ironically, it's her husband whom she worshipped who has shat on her. I love the way she always pulls through, no matter what. I also like the way the maternal instinct comes out with Denny and the younger ones. I like the way she schemes and she plots and I like the way she thinks – I love her humour. I wouldn't want to cross her but I respect her a great deal. Even when she does get scary or tells people off, it is usually for their

people. Just because you're in prison, it doesn't make you a certain "type". They are just people who have made mistakes and face the consequences.'

Despite her enormously varied and highly successful career, Henry had never been nominated for an award until *Bad Girls* at last year's National Television Awards. 'What I think overwhelmed me the most then was seeing all these people waiting in the rain for six hours to see us. I got really choked. You don't think of yourself like that. It's a job, a wonderful job we are privileged to do and get paid for, but you don't think that people think they really love you.'

Henry says being recognised in the street is, on the whole, lovely. 'I love getting fan mail and I always reply, and it is so nice when people appreciate your work,' she enthuses. 'And I still get star-struck too. I saw Vera and Jack Duckworth at the awards and I was pissing my knickers!'

The most star-struck Henry ever got was when she was at drama school and was Frank Finlay's dresser for a play he was doing. 'I met so many people: Kirk Douglas, Charlton Heston, Laurence Olivier, and Frank Finlay knew I liked Laurence Olivier. We went to a party after the show and Laurence Olivier came up to me and said: "I hear you think I'm the best thing since sliced bread." I just had to run off to the toilet. And the next day, there was a parcel in Frank's dressing room for me and it was full of pictures

own good; it's not always for selfish reasons.'

Henry beams with pride when she talks of Yvonne, like a proud parent. Which, one supposes, she is. 'Yvonne knows she's got to do the time because she did something wrong, was caught and found guilty. She accepts that. Even in prison, though, I wouldn't put anything past her; there's nothing I think she couldn't achieve. She's prison royalty.'

Bad Girls isn't Henry's first experience of prison life. She worked in HMP Holloway when she was at the National Theatre and learned a lot about women's prisons there. 'We weren't allowed to ask the inmates questions but if they said things about themselves, we could listen. I worked there for about four months and, at the end of it, the women did a play. It was quite an experience.'

Hence, Henry didn't feel the need to go back into prison to research her role. Part of that was due to the quality of the writing and part was because: 'I didn't want to get preconceived ideas, go into prison, meet a prisoner and say "That's Yvonne" because you can't do that. People are people and it's their circumstances that are different. I don't think you can stereotype

'I still get star-struck too'

Laurence Olivier had signed for me. That was amazing, quite the fulfilled ambition.'

Today, Henry still has unfulfilled ambitions but you get the feeling they won't stay that way for long. As well as winning an award of her very own, she wants her daughter to grow up happy ('She's seven and in love with Jack Ellis at the moment, so that's a bit worrying'), and she wants to continue doing work she enjoys. For the foreseeable future, that can only mean *Bad Girls*.

Sharon Duncan-Brewster

Sharon Duncan-Brewster has taken to changing her hairstyle and telling people she is her sister. The twenty-five-year-old actress hasn't developed a bizarre personality disorder: it's just that she's a bit shy. 'I get recognised in the weirdest places,' she laughs. 'I've been asked for autographs in Sainsbury's and I've been in Ikea, lugging heavy, awkward furniture around, and someone has come up to me and said "You're Crystal, innit?" And the last time I went out to a club, it was unbelievable.'

Duncan-Brewster tells the story of her night out, almost unable to contain her own disbelief. 'I went to a gay club in London to see someone playing live and loads of people kept coming up to me and asking if I was Crystal. I started off saying "No, that's my sister", because I was so awe-struck by the whole thing. Everyone was shouting across the bar, "It's you, innit?" which was nice but a bit weird.'

'Everyone was shouting across the bar. "It's you, innit?"'

Duncan-Brewster says she loves the appreciation of the fans but, sometimes, it gets a bit too much for her. 'Some nights, you just want to chill out and be on your own. That particular night out was fine. The show has been really successful on the gay scene and I think, first time round, they were the most supportive people. I think because of them and some others, the second series was even more popular.'

Then there's the hair. Recently, this has been making Duncan-Brewster even more recognisable to her fans. 'I had taken to changing my hairstyle every two months and, in the play I last did, it was really soft and straight. I looked completely different to Crystal, so people only did a double-take and kept walking. Only the gutsy ones come up and speak to you. Now I've got long plaits back in, I can't hide so easily.'

Despite her shyness at being recognised, Duncan-Brewster loves playing the role of Crystal: 'The religious kleptomaniac. Bible in one hand, guitar in the other – and stolen stuff stashed about her person, fantastic! She is so different to me that I love playing her. I have a religious background – my mum is very religious and my dad goes to church – and, like her, I'm from East London and have Trinidad and Tobago parentage but that's about it. She's hard-core Christian.'

Duncan-Brewster, who trained at the renowned Anna Scher Children's Theatre, thinks it's great to see a character like Crystal on television. She was, however, concerned once Crystal had served her sentence and was released: 'I didn't know what was going to happen at all. I thought they could either get new characters in, she could re-offend or they might show her life outside. Luckily, they got her back, so that's good. I appreciate I am in a brilliant drama and that's all that I ever wanted, really: to be in a TV show that's well-known and have a character that's different. I've always played prostitutes, drug dealers, bad girls, so it's nice to play something with a bit more depth.'

As well as playing prostitutes and drug dealers, Duncan-Brewster has a distinguished theatrical background and has had roles in award-winning plays such as Sarah Kane's *Crave*

and Rebecca Prichard's acclaimed *Yard Gal*, at London's Royal Court Theatre, where she was spotted for *Bad Girls*. Not only was her acting in the play hailed for managing to make the character, Boo, ring utterly true, but the play was also transferred to New York.

Duncan-Brewster explains: 'We had talked about it going all over, to Canada and Australia, but when they said New York wanted it, it was the best news. We were, like, "Yahoo!" There were just two of us in the play and we had such a wicked time there. All the songs say the city never sleeps and they're not wrong: it's alive. We'd finish the show and go to a bar then on to a club or a restaurant. They didn't close until the early morning and we didn't have to be at work until half seven at night, so it was pretty wild. We were naughty every night.' There's a glint in

Duncan-Brewster's eyes, of which Crystal would certainly disapprove.

As well as acting, Duncan-Brewster has been cultivating her musical talents, which have been at the fore of *Bad Girls* ever since programme producer Brian Park found out she could sing and play guitar. 'They never knew to begin with and I didn't think they would care either, but when Crystal sang "Amazing Grace" after Rachel Hicks died, I got a phone call saying Brian really liked it and wanted to close the episode with it, over the closing credits and everything. My mum was well proud.'

Duncan-Brewster continues her musical exploits away from the *Bad Girls* set, too. She is writing her own songs as well as singing as part of a band. 'I jam with some people about once a week and write songs and stuff. That's really good too. What with that, work and my other hobby – photography – I'm keeping pretty busy.'

The actress is not, however, so busy that she doesn't harbour any other ambitions: 'I would love to be in the movies,' she purrs. 'Quality British movies. I'd love to work with Mike Leigh; I think he's fantastic. Or Guy Ritchie – he'd do. And I'd love to do some Shakespeare at the RSC. That would be a real challenge.'

In the meantime, Duncan-Brewster is more than happy playing a religious kleptomaniac. 'I

There's a glint in Duncan-Brewster's eyes, of which Crystal would certainly disapprove

mean,' she giggles. 'Who wouldn't want to play opposite Nathan?' Certainly, the actor who plays Josh should be flattered. 'He is a good-looking bloke!' continues Duncan-Brewster, laughing. Crystal would, at least, agree with this.

Victoria Alcock

It's official: Victoria Alcock has street cred. Official according to her nephews, at least: 'One is ten and the other is twenty-two and, now, I'm no longer just Auntie Victoria. Now, I'm one of the Julies in *Bad Girls*. They're both proud of me.'

Before she attended the *Bad Girls* audition, however, Alcock was excited at the thought of playing a baddie. 'I've always wanted to play a baddie so I got really excited. I thought: 'I can do hard, I can do tough,' and it wasn't until I got there, I realised I was going up to play a nutter. They asked: 'Can you read for one of the Julies?' I was quite happy doing that and I think you have to do what you're naturally capable of doing. I don't suppose I'm a tough nut.'

Now, Alcock says she wouldn't swap Julie S. for the world. 'She's been in a lot of scrapes but I think she almost always comes out on top, though not without a little heartbreak.' Although Alcock loves playing alongside Kika Myralees' Julie J., she has also enjoyed the time spent away from her in the third series. 'It was a bit strange without her there beside me, but acting with Ian Dunn who plays my ex, Trevor, was wonderful, a real departure. Seeing Jane Lowe, who plays Monica, again was marvellous, too, as was finally meeting little David, Julie's son. He's real!' she cackles.

Bad Girls isn't the first time Alcock has worked on a predominantly female set. As Agnes in *The House of Eliot*, she was surrounded by the ladies of the dramatic fashion house. There is, coincidentally, a pattern forming: that of Alcock playing characters famed for their dressmaking abilities. With her mother a professional dressmaker, is this also one of her talents? 'Absolutely not!' she says emphatically. 'I am hopeless. I would love to say I was good at it just to please my mother (who used to complain that I was sewing wrongly on *The House of Eliot*) but I can't. She's teaching me to knit just now, so

'I don't suppose I'm a tough nut'

that's an indication of how proficient I am.'

Alcock's talents lie in other directions. She is an accomplished horsewoman who has been riding since she was four years old and she is also a qualified fitness instructor. 'It's great to have another string to your bow. Kika is a fantastic cook, for example. I have tasted her cheesecake and it is so delicious, you would fight your best mate for it.'

Immensely proud of *Bad Girls* herself, Alcock's last claim to fame was as the woman who came forward and shopped *Coronation Street*'s Jon Lindsay as a fraudster and a bigamist. 'That's right,' she says, 'I saved Deirdre from prison. I was the saviour of the nation, as the papers said at the time.' She giggles to herself, perhaps thinking of the street cred.

Kika Myralees

Kika Myralees couldn't be less like Julie J.: well-spoken and elegant with not a hint of a peculiar hairstyle, it is testimony to Myralees' acting ability that her transformation is so convincing. 'She is such a great character to play,' the actress enthuses. 'I must say I wouldn't have chosen me to play the part – I normally play frightfully posh women.' Much to her surprise, however, Myralees was cast alongside Victoria Alcock: 'When I went for the audition, there were five girls there and we each had to go into the audition in different combinations. When Victoria and I went in, it just clicked.'

Myralees enjoys the closeness of working with Alcock, arguing that the Julies' behaviour isn't that strange: 'It was a bit odd doing the echoing thing to start with but now I understand. I do it with friends of mine, I think it's something we all do to some degree.' Nor, she argues, are the Julies mere comic relief: 'Like all the other characters in the series, they are more rounded than that. In the second series especially, the story of having the children taken away was very important – and an issue that affects a lot of women in prison.'

Strangely, playing Julie J. lends Myralees anonymity, something in which she revels. 'I can sit next to the other Julie on a train and no one will recognise me. Fame simply doesn't interest me. If I were younger, I might enjoy it or want it more but now I'm not bothered. I did all that kind of thing when I was young.' Indeed she did.

'Fame simply doesn't interest me'

When Myralees was younger, before she was in *The Darling Buds of May* or *Strathblair* or *Red Dwarf*, she was a singer in a band: 'We were called Danny And The No-Goodniks and The Pogues supported us once. I sang terribly badly but I mostly did ironic dancing.'

These days, Myralees' life isn't all sex, drugs and rock-and-roll. Rather, it's countryside and caring for her horse. She's also halfway through a degree with the Open University: 'I lived in London for fifteen years and eventually I decided enough was enough. I moved out to the country, where my horse was, and I simply adore it.'

Myralees was born in Germany, lived in Scotland (she is descended from Robert Louis Stevenson) and now lives in Surrey. She calls herself a traveller and says she would love to spend half her year in Europe and half here.

For the moment, however, Myralees is content. 'Work isn't always about doing something terribly meaningful or life-changing or provocative. Whatever you do, you must do it with your integrity and pride: it doesn't matter what it is, you do your best.' Myralees smiles and, for an instant, there is a glimpse of Julie J.'s compassion and goodness. They are not so different after all. Apart from the hairclips, of course.

Lara Cazalet

'I remember the day after the first episode I was in got aired; I was shouted at by some workmen, asking if I was the one on smack. It's not the sort thing you expect builders to shout at you, is it?' In fact, Lara Cazalet scrubs up pretty well when she's not playing a drug-addicted prisoner called Zandra Plackett. Devoid of skin complexion issues and the multitude of problems that plagued the ill-fated Zandra, she is also full of bouncing energy and good humour.

So, why would Cazalet want to play this sort of character? She laughs, 'I actually grew up wanting to be a singer. So I went through the traditional path of various musicals and gradually realised that I preferred the acting bits where I was speaking and not singing.' Music's loss was drama's gain. Not many actors could have portrayed such an emotional gamut; Zandra's incident-filled time behind bars took her from heroin dependency to being dumped by a boyfriend whilst inside, still holding the baby (in her case, whilst on a roof). All this before being diagnosed with a terminal brain tumour.

Didn't Cazalet find playing Zandra daunting – or at least a little depressing? 'Well, yes, sometimes. On occasions, I would spend the entire day on set maintaining a level of emotional intensity, just to keep the momentum up for a twelve-hour shoot. But, having said that, there were a lot of laughs as well and I could always put it away at the end of the day – with everything that Zandra endured, you couldn't not. Besides, I'm a relaxed and, I would say, pretty happy person.'

Indeed, Cazalet strikes you immediately as an immensely warm and considerate person. She is one of those rare people who only says nice things about other people and her words are always accompanied by a ready laugh. Quite the opposite the character she played, particularly when Zandra first entered Larkhall. 'I wouldn't

particularly be drawn to Zandra in the first series,' she says diplomatically. 'She was so full of anger and incredibly selfish. She manipulated people, though much of her behaviour was fuelled by drugs that just controlled her every waking thought. But, by Series Two, she was much more trusting and open. I loved playing the scenes with Crystal. They were so tender and it was brilliant that she had just one person she could completely rely on – who really knew her before she died.'

Playing out her character's death proved difficult. 'My family couldn't watch when it was on. It was very eerie to perform it, as they shot the memorial scenes whilst I was still on set: I watched my own eulogy.' Never one to be kept down, though, Cazalet did try to sneak back in. 'I did try it on,' she chuckles. 'I tiptoed into the servery in one shot – just in the background – but tripped over quite dramatically and the director caught me and ordered me off set. I thought we could justify it as Zandra having come back to haunt Larkhall, which is probably something she would try to do.'

Cazalet muses: 'If I could come back as another character it would probably have to be Shell. She's dangerous but quite incompetent. She's one of those characters that can be funny without meaning to be. But there's so many cool characters that I'd have liked to get stuck into

'I was shouted at by some workmen, asking if I was the one on smack'

she bought? 'Lots of things – television and theatre. I'd already done two guest parts on *The Bill*, so that's probably the only avenue that can no longer be explored. I'm very optimistic about the future: I like variety. In fact, I've just got back from an episode of *A & E*.' She also indulges in a little jazz singing with her brother. She has plenty to keep her busy in her leisure time: 'I like yoga to relax and I also play the piano. Generally, though, I'm very gregarious – I like spending time with people and socialising.'

Wherever the future takes Cazalet, *Bad Girls* will, of course, always be a part of her – not least because its legion of fans remember her with such fondness. Cazalet smiles: 'I have had some amazing letters. The sort of letters that make you so glad to have been part of something that has obviously affected so many people in a very real way.' Zandra's classic lines and her unique vocabulary will also be quoted and remembered by fans for many years to come, and the emotional roller coaster she took everyone on is still fresh in people's memories.

Yet, despite the success of her character portrayal, Cazalet is devoid of any show-business airs and graces. She confesses: 'When we were nominated for the National TV Awards, I panicked over a dress. In the end, a friend lent

– though I'm more than happy with Zandra. Besides, all of the characters were brilliantly cast – everyone's great at what they do.'

Cazalet describes the background research she did for the part of Zandra. 'I visited a drop-in centre in Kingston, a halfway house, Holloway and a drug rehabilitation centre. When you are covering such serious issues, you want to get them right,' she explains. 'Being on a show like this really opens your eyes to the sort of things that you don't normally have to think about. But I will remember my time on the show with only fondness. I've made loads of good friends in the process and we had a ball.' She raises the scarf she's wearing: 'Brian Park bought this for me as a leaving present. After my last scene, he wheeled in a TV and they had edited together some of my "finest moments". It was amazing – everyone was so lovely.'

So what next for the woman who describes her favourite animal as a tiger cub and openly confesses to Kajagoogoo being the first record

'Being on a show like this really opens your eyes to the sort of things that you don't normally have to think about'

me a long, sparkling red skirt that I carted around in the bottom of my bag for a week. I had no idea until afterwards, it was worth several thousand pounds! Still, I had teamed it with a top that only cost fourteen quid. I don't think you can tell...can you?'

Tracey Wilkinson

There was a time when Tracey Wilkinson didn't want to be an actress. In fact, had she stuck to her original career plan, she would never have seen the inside of HMP Larkhall, never mind appearing in the likes of *Billy Elliot*, *Our Friends in the North* and *Hillsborough*. Instead, she'd be an expert on knitting patterns in the north-east of England, where she grew up.

'I wanted to be a journalist,' she confesses. 'There was something about it that really attracted me when I was at school and I spent eight weeks doing work experience on the *Shields Gazette*. When I left, they said they would see me through journalism college and give me a job afterwards. I remember being very excited at the time.' The excitement didn't last, however, and after a stint in youth theatre, Wilkinson was set on pursuing another path. 'No offence to the *Shields Gazette* but if I had gone there, I think I'd either be writing about knitting on the women's page or reporting from court on someone stealing tins of beans.'

'For a lot of working-class kids, theatre was another form of education and, certainly for me, an expression of political leanings. By the time I had been in youth theatre for three months, I had completely changed my mind.'

Wilkinson's first professional job came immediately after she left drama school in Manchester. 'At the end of the course, it was customary for all the final-year students to do their audition pieces in front of an audience. I came on and did my bits and one of the bookers from *Coronation Street* was there. She came up to me afterwards and said: 'Well, we're supposed to have a delivery boy but I suppose it could be a girl. Could you do it next week?' So I delivered a bunch of flowers to Mavis Riley that got her and Derek together. It was only seven lines but I was pretty chuffed with it.'

This was the beginning of the journey that led to the role of Di Barker, the nice but strange prison officer on G-Wing, HMP Larkhall. 'From her first appearance, there have been clues that there is a lot of pressure on Di and she isn't as capable of coping with it as she might be. Her job is stressful and she has been caring for her invalid mother for some time and, after developing a mild form of erotomania focused on Dominic, it is quite evident that she's teetering on the edge of a nervous breakdown.'

> 'there is a lot of pressure on Di and she isn't as capable of coping with it as she might be'

And quite a serious, prolonged one at that. Some of the warning signs of a breakdown are fixations, violence and strange preoccupations.

Wilkinson's career seems to be peppered with the strange and the bizarre. The most unusual was a job she got in Canada: 'I went on a foreign artist's visiting grant, to work on a show about genetic engineering,' she chuckles. 'We rehearsed in a farmhouse on Wolf Island, in the middle of Lake Ontario, then we toured with ten Clydesdale horses, four outriding horses, four caravans and a huge circus tent. We did that for seven months, all over Canada. It would take a week to get from venue to venue because we could only do ten miles a day with the Clydesdales. You'd see all the posh Canadian cars zooming past and the drivers doing double-takes at us. It was quite a hoot.'

Wilkinson, it would seem, is mistress of understatement. She is quite diffident about her varied career, which has included theatrical stints at the Royal Court and the National Theatre, the latter of which saw her perform in the premiere

of Jonathan Harvey's play, *Guiding Star*. Wilkinson admits a genuine love of treading the boards. 'For a long time, I didn't have any enthusiasm for television because the kind of parts I was being offered then – nurses or messengers – were very dull. In theatre, I was playing leads or second leads and, even though the money isn't as good, it was more exciting to be playing leads in theatre than saying: "The doctor will be along to see you in a minute" on TV.'

Of course, a role like Di Barker was too good to miss and the interview she had with producer Brian Park only fortified her belief that she was right for the role. 'I really enjoyed meeting Brian and, if you enjoy meeting someone, you're much more relaxed and you're much more yourself. When I came in for a recall and met the director and Brian, he directed me through a scene, saying: "Can you be happy in this bit, pensive in this bit and troubled in this bit?" Essentially, I gurned my way through a scene and got the job.'

Thanks to her gurning, not to mention her considerable acting talent, Wilkinson landed the part of Di and, from the outset, sought to do the character justice. 'One of my premises when I started with Di was that, for her, freedom is at work and prison is at home. That was a parallel

'Essentially, I gurned my way through a scene and got the job'

I was really aware of and wanted to play. Also, it's important that Di Barker isn't just stupid and mad. It's vital you see that there is pressure on being in this environment and the strain of looking after an elderly relative. There's a caring, nurturing side to her but there are too many demands on Di, especially as she is coping alone. I think Di is aware that she has certain tendencies that could stick her in prison as well.'

Playing a role as emotionally demanding as Di Barker, Wilkinson says her relaxation time is extremely precious. When she's not sailing, walking or horseriding, Wilkinson enjoys horseracing ('I used to follow the form') and

going to the dogs. She is also writing a screenplay with a friend and the pair have been invited to apply for the prestigious Dennis Potter Screenwriting Award.

Then there's the football. As you might expect from a lass from between Sunderland and Newcastle, Wilkinson loves football: 'I'll watch any old team play – Sunday league and I'm there – but I am a Sunderland fan. Last year, I was a member of Wimbledon Football Club because it was an excuse to go and see premier-league football, but some of my best memories are of watching Sunderland play. I remember when they won the Cup in 1973, and everyone running up and down their garden paths shouting: 'We've scored!' and the whisky being brought out, and then running back in to see the rest of the match. It was great.'

Now a team player herself, Wilkinson loves the atmosphere on the *Bad Girls* set. 'I was very nervous joining after the first series, with everyone knowing each other, but they really are a welcoming, embracing ensemble who are here to enjoy themselves. I find that working with a group of women is an absolute joy though, obviously, I think Di should have her own spin-off series!' Wilkinson laughs, the slightest lilt of a north-east accent betraying her mischievousness.

Lindsey Fawcett

From playing the world's favourite orphan, Annie, to being baby-faced, multiple murderer Shaz Wylie, Lindsey Fawcett's career is nothing if not diverse. 'I had ringlets and everything!' she says, obviously aware how hard this is to imagine, now she has a bleached blonde crop. 'It was only an amateur production but, from then, I knew acting was the way forward.'

So determined was Fawcett to follow her ambition, that she tried to pursue acting as part of her work experience whilst at school. That avenue wasn't available, so she opted for learning about casting instead. 'I went to the Sheffield Crucible and met Wendy, the casting director, there. She was fantastic, quite inspirational, and I learned a lot. After I had gone back to school after my work experience, we kept in touch and, when she got a job at the National Theatre in London, I got the part of Bet in *Oliver!* at the Palladium.'

That was Fawcett's first big break. Wendy helped her get an agent and, soon, Fawcett appeared in *The Prime of Miss Jean Brodie* at the National Theatre and as Scout in *To Kill A Mockingbird*. And all this without even attending drama school. 'I think you learn something more by just doing it than being taught it. I know that's the case with me.' Fawcett has worked with great actors, writers and directors, including Alan Ayckbourn, whose play, *Dreaming Callisto Seven*, Fawcett appeared in, both in the West End and in several productions at the Sheffield Crucible.

London's glittering West End is a far cry from Fawcett's home in Stocksbridge, outside Sheffield, but, even now, the young actress doesn't let London's bright lights seduce her. 'I still live at home because I like it. I love Sheffield and I like being close to my family. Actually, I like anywhere that's not London. I like cities but I find London too fast. I'm quite a laid-back person, so the frenetic pace is too exhausting for me – I'd prefer to sit in front of the box and

quietly idle away a few hours.' Her dedication to watching television is demonstrated by her uncanny impression of Grampa in *The Simpsons* – it is inspiring to watch such a petite and dainty creature emanate such a sound. But Fawcett is full of such surprises.

Despite her reservations about working in London, Fawcett is happy to do so now, such is her enjoyment of working on *Bad Girls*. She found the team – both cast and crew – made her feel at once like one of the family. 'On my first day's filming, I didn't have a clue where I was going but the minute I walked on set, one of the crew saw me and said, "You must be playing Shaz." I was just how they had expected me to look, which was a great feeling.'

Shaz's 'look' didn't perturb the previously ringleted actress one bit. She got the audition for *Bad Girls* in a week when she had already had

'I wouldn't be friends with her because I think she would do my head in'

six other auditions and, although she hadn't seen the first series due to work commitments, it was a show in which she was interested. 'Even then, I never realised how popular it was. I had seen clips and visited the website, so slowly I came to terms with the incredible following it had. I knew it was something I wanted to work on so, in the audition, when Brian Park asked me if I would mind having my hair cropped and dyed, I thought what the hell and said yes. That was that, really.'

That was indeed that, and Shaz was born. Fawcett insists that she and Shaz share few characteristics, particularly not her homicidal tendencies. 'I am impulsive but much more thoughtful than Shaz, and I don't think I need attention as much as she obviously does. To be honest, she would be too much for me. I wouldn't be friends with her because I think she would do my head in. I think she'd be fun to go out and get drunk with but if I had to spend any amount of time with her, I'd go mad. It's like she's on speed or something!'

For the part, Fawcett did a lot of research since she knew nothing of what went on inside prison before *Bad Girls*. 'I think that's a problem with society in general: nobody really has a carefully considered opinion on prisons. If you don't actively go and look for information on prison – and I wouldn't have if I hadn't been doing this – you don't have an opinion on it. We put people away and we forget about them.'

It was a particular challenge for Fawcett to play a young killer, so she read *Cries Unheard* by Gitta Sereny. This is the story of Mary Bell, who killed two children when she was still a child herself. 'It was a revelation. I learned so many things I never knew and thought about so many things I had never considered before. Poor Mary Bell didn't know what was happening when she was institutionalised because she was so young, and no one really explained things to her. With Shaz, she is supposed to be seventeen but she is very young for her age. I think the issue of young people and the effect of being in prison is very topical.'

As well as raising serious issues, playing Shaz is great fun too. 'It's not often you can say you have fun with everyone at work but I can genuinely say that about *Bad Girls*. Alicya and I muck about in much the same ways as Shaz and Denny and some of the things we've had to do have been brilliant. I loved the scenes we did

'I'd love to play Bodybag. That would be a blast'

with the tongue-piercing; it was so mad. And I like the singing I get to do too.'

With a role as rewarding, complex and ripe for development as Shaz, twenty-two-year-old Fawcett couldn't be happier. She does harbour a secret yearning, however: 'If I could, through the magic of television, I'd love to play Bodybag. That would be a blast. Or Shell. I'd really like to get my teeth into her too…'

Isabelle Amyes

You could call Isabelle Amyes' first day as Barbara Hunt a baptism of fire. No sooner had she donned her signature half-moon glasses, than she was being wrestled to the floor, kicking and screaming. 'I suppose it's one of those moments when you ask what you've let yourself in for,' she smiles. 'But there is only one way to approach these things and that is to really go for it and not care what you look like, so I just unleashed this torrent of emotion. I think it worked because it looked all right on screen, though I was exhausted afterwards.'

Amyes, whose face regularly crinkles into a delicious mischievous grin, hails from a theatrical family. Her father, Julian Amyes, was the actor-turned-director, turned Head of Drama for Granada TV, while her mother, Anne Allan, was an actress and writer. Her parents proved to be great inspirational figures in her life. 'My father came to see me in an early role and gave me a strong lecture on the importance of being truthful when acting; I've never forgotten it. And, besides, a studio has always felt like home.'

When Amyes first approached Barbara's story, she was extremely courageous in the honesty she brought to the role; it had been only a matter of months since her mother had died of cancer when she was offered the part. Barbara, of course, has been sentenced to three years for the mercy-killing of her cancer-stricken husband, Peter. 'It was a very emotional time,' Amyes confesses. 'I had a heightened awareness of losing someone very dear to such a debilitating and cruel disease'. It is testimony to her strength as a person and as an actress that she didn't flinch from tackling something so personal and potentially demoralising. 'In actuality it was, I suppose, cathartic. Besides, I could see from the outset that I was working with a hugely supportive cast and crew.'

Amyes tells of her initial reaction to the *Bad Girls* set. 'When I started, I didn't want to come on set before my first day because I wanted to be as awe-struck as Barbara would have been when she first arrived at prison.' She wasn't disappointed. 'The enormity of the set just overwhelmed me. It was just so huge and it felt so much like an institution. It was oppressive and towering, grubby and menacing. It made me sure I would never break the law – I know I couldn't cope with being in prison for real.'

An accomplished writer herself, Amyes shares an enormous respect for the writers of the show. 'They really imbue the programme with a heart.

'I didn't want to come on set before my first day because I wanted to be as awe-struck as Barbara would have been'

Sometimes that is missing in drama but, here, the atmosphere is alive and everyone gives one hundred per cent.'

Amyes may have initially been worried about joining the cast in the second series, but she soon found her concerns were groundless. 'I did worry that it could have been very cliquey on set but, actually, everyone is wonderful. You couldn't hope to work with a better cast. To be honest, it's a bit like being back at school (I went to an all girls' school), only without the silly, childish goings on. Everyone on set – cast and crew – make coming to work a joy.' Has *Bad*

was she. Amyes concedes it takes a lot to faze her and attributes her repose to her theatrical upbringing: 'I think when you grow up with it, you do tend to cope with it better. I am also contented and happy in my own life, so I feel able to confront and embrace dramatic storylines. I can return to "me" afterwards. It's actually quite therapeutic.'

Amyes immediately strikes you as someone with a mind that rarely shuts down. And that mischievous grin of hers often breaks into a deep, growling chuckle; she obviously enjoys life. So how does she relax and recuperate from her day job as a Larkhall resident? 'It's the standard cliché for actresses to say they like cooking, so I feel compelled to come up with something more outlandish,' she laughs. 'But I do really like cooking and preparing dinner parties. Oh, and opera. I love opera – all those soaring crescendos and the rhythm of the lyrics.' Words are something that are close to Amyes's heart, it transpires. 'I always have a thesaurus to hand. I've always been fascinated by words, which is one of the main reasons I love to write.'

Indeed, she has recently finished scribing a film with a writing partner. But there is no immediate danger of Larkhall losing her to an artist's garret somewhere, especially as Barbara's situation has been made more complex by the revelation that she is a bigamist. 'That was quite a surprise!' she laughs.

'To be honest, it's a bit like being back at school'

Despite the fact that Barbara hasn't been entirely honest with her fellow inmates, Amyes still has huge admiration for her character: 'I think she is honourable. She did what she did out of love for Peter, not for material gain. When I went for the audition, Brian Park told me Barbara and Peter met on a tube and they were instantly attracted to one another. She was quite besotted by him and, if anything, was led astray by love. I can understand that.'

Girls' popularity made this even better? 'Oh, absolutely,' Amyes enthuses. 'People are so very nice about it.'

Amyes brings a quiet but powerful rectitude to Barbara; a sense of dignity in undignified surroundings, where grown women are often treated like children. She admits that her favourite storyline is when she prepares a 'herbal' remedy for the ailing Zandra. 'It shows that Barbara is a woman with her own mind and her own very strong moral code. She puts a lot on the line when she thinks something is important. I have a lot of respect and empathy for her.'

It's a continuing presence of sanity and pragmatism that has won the character many sympathisers. 'She doesn't fit anyone's profile of a prisoner. She is an ordinary woman who has had to struggle with overwhelming circumstances,' Amyes emphasises with a thoughtful nod. 'Hurt breeds hurt and, in Barbara's world, nothing has been gained by her incarceration apart from bitterness and loss of faith in a brutal and impersonal system.'

An actor with whom Amyes once worked remarked that it was as though she acted inside a big, pink bubble, so cool, calm and collected

Nathan Constance

Before he got the part as Josh Mitchell in *Bad Girls*, Nathan Constance was best known as one of 'Harchester United's' star players in the Sky One football drama, *Dream Team*. Needless to say, he suffered quite a culture shock in transferring from a male-dominated drama to a female one. 'When I came into *Bad Girls*, I was in the minority – it was very intimidating,' he stifles a bashful laugh. 'I'm not great at talking to women at the best of times but when there are twenty of them in the room...!'

Born and bred in Ilford, Essex, Constance has worked extremely hard to become an actor. He got a part in the musical *Carmen Jones* when he was thirteen: 'That meant I needed Wednesdays off school for matinees and weeks off for rehearsals. My school said there was no way that could happen so I went to Sylvia Young (who owns a renowned stage school), she gave me a scholarship and I started going to school there.'

The journey to his new school in Marylebone took Constance one-and-a-half hours every morning. With amazing support from his mum, and through his own hard work, the effort paid off and it wasn't long before Constance was landing parts in *The Bill* and *London's Burning*. By fourteen, he had a part in the children's drama set in a stage school, *The Biz*. Constance stayed with the series for three years and then got a part in *Dream Team*, which in turn led to *Bad Girls*.

Constance couldn't be happier playing Josh Mitchell, especially as Josh is more than the

'To play someone with all that energy, someone who makes other people smile, is great'

typical cheeky chappie: 'As the series progresses, his character develops a lot and the story follows him more.' Not only that, but playing Josh means Constance gets to smile: 'Normally, I frown a lot. I play serious characters, like the guy with the chip on his shoulder, so it's really good to finally play someone who is the life and soul of the party. To play someone with all that energy, someone who makes other people smile, is great.'

Recently, Constance has also had a chance to act in a couple of films: *Wonderland*, directed by Michael Winterbottom, and *A Kind of Hush*. Film is a passion for Constance but he finds it impossible to name his favourite: 'It's A Wonderful Life is fantastic but then so is Beverly Hills Cop.'

While Constance brings a lot to the character of Josh Mitchell, there is something he doesn't: his DIY skills. 'I am hopeless at DIY,' he guffaws, 'absolutely terrible. If I tried to fix a pipe, there would be disaster. It's just as well Josh is a better handyman than me, considering how often something is broken in that prison. If he weren't, the place would have no electricity and be knee-deep in water.' And he always looks so capable with his tool bag. Now that's acting.

Roland Oliver

Almost the proudest moment of Roland Oliver's acting career occurred during the first series of *Bad Girls*: 'Simon Stubberfield was playing golf with Jim Fenner and I had to sink a putt. It was about a ten-foot putt and I did it in one take. I got a standing ovation from the crew but no one was more surprised than me.'

Oliver has a long and distinguished career as an actor behind him. After a couple of years in the National Youth Theatre, he studied English at Oxford, where he once again dabbled with performing. 'When I was a small boy, I wanted to be a professional cricketer and, after that, I had ambitions to be a barrister, though, with the latter, I think it was the

'What man of my age wouldn't enjoy a job which meant being surrounded by attractive and pleasant young women all day?'

showy part of it that appealed – standing up, swaying the jury with impassioned rhetoric.' As it was, his first professional job in showbusiness was as an assistant stage manager in 1966. It was enough to get Oliver hooked and, for the next fifteen years, he toured theatres across the country.

'I spent a lot of time in Scotland, working at the Traverse and the Royal Lyceum Theatres in Edinburgh. I always harboured a desire to be a classical actor, but one of the happiest times of my working life was doing new plays. Being the first person to create a role is pretty stimulating,' he recalls.

In 1980, Oliver landed a major television role, in *Dr Who*. After that, parts followed in *Bergerac*, *Juliet Bravo*, *The Bill*, *Inspector Morse* and *Rumpole of the Bailey*. 'I'm one of those actors who's been in almost everything you can think of without ever having a major role. I've played Tory MPs, solicitors, magistrates and I played a prison governor before, in *London's Burning*.'

Oliver enjoys playing Stubberfield – 'What man of my age wouldn't enjoy a job which meant being surrounded by attractive and pleasant young women all day?' – but he considers himself a

theatre actor at heart. 'That's what I went into the business for and that's what interests me the most: developing a character in action and working with a director in rehearsals.'

As for his character in *Bad Girls*, Oliver is sympathetic. 'I think he wants a quiet life and that is probably not the best credential for being a prison governor. I think we can safely say he's getting away with the top job rather than in command of it. He seems to be a fairly honest person who is loyal to his colleagues, rather unwisely so in the case of Jim Fenner.' Oliver laughs. 'One guy who knows me said, only half-jokingly, "You really ought to sort that Jim Fenner out, you know. He's really not behaving properly at all." I suppose he might have a point!'

Jane Lowe

People scream at Jane Lowe in the street. 'It's mostly teenagers who scream at me and jump up and down: "Are you Monica?" they ask. I explain I was but I'm not in *Bad Girls* any more, but they don't care. "Tell us all about it, we love it, we wouldn't miss it." People are strange sometimes, aren't they?'

From her tone, it would be safe to say that Lowe finds such public displays of affection quite bewildering. Monica was a major character in series one but was let out at the end. She reappears in series three, when her halfway house becomes a temporary home to an electronically tagged Julie S. Lowe didn't work on the show or appear on screen for over a year, yet Monica still looms large in *Bad Girls* mythology.

'When I did the scenes in the halfway house, it was like coming home,' she enthuses. 'Seeing the girls again was rather marvellous. A lot of the crew was the same, too, so it was nice to see everyone. I didn't miss the prison though. That set is such a terrific set but it is so imposing, so frightening.' Lowe pauses. 'Come to think of it, Monica would be missing the girls too.'

Not that Jane Lowe and Monica Lindsay have that much in common. Lowe says that playing the buttoned up, middle-class Monica was a wonderful opportunity: 'She had so much to deal with,' she says. 'Spencer, her Down's Syndrome son, the learning curve of getting used to prison life, Spencer's death and his funeral, and finally getting out at the end: she really ran the gamut of emotions.'

But, contrary to what you might think, Lowe doesn't share Lindsay's middle-class background. 'She was one of the only middle-class parts I have played in a career that has spanned thirty-

'That set is such a terrific set but it is so imposing, so frightening'

five years; I'm actually a working-class girl from Lancashire. I've just finished an episode in *Heartbeat* playing a clairvoyant cleaner, and that was much more me than Monica.'

Lowe grew up in Wigan, where she always harboured acting ambitions but didn't pursue them, at least initially. 'In those days, Wigan was a coal-and-cotton town and it was difficult to tell anyone that you wanted to be something as poncey as an actress.' Lowe, however, eventually decided that she did want to act and, since then, has played parts from saints (Saint Joan, to be precise) to sinners such as Lady Macbeth.

It is this variety of work that Lowe relishes, even if precariousness comes as part of the package. 'Last summer, I did a play in London in which I played an Argentinian whore. You can't get further removed from Monica Lindsay than that. I had a cleavage down to my waist, a miniskirt, plastered in make-up with this mane of black hair. That's the joy of acting, you don't know what you're going to be doing next.'

Lisa Turner

Lisa Turner didn't think she was anything like Gina Rossi – until she described the feisty P.O. to others: 'In television, you often get cast quite close to your type, so I thought it was nice not playing to type. But having said that, there have been moments when I've described Gina to other people and I realise that I am a bit like her. Not a lot, mind.'

Turner could do a lot worse than sharing some of her character's attributes. The actress says she not only likes playing Gina, she likes Gina as a person, too: 'I'm still getting to know her myself, but there's no doubt she's a real firebrand. She's got a bit of a mouth on her – she calls a spade a spade – and she acts on instinct, even when she knows it's the wrong thing to do. She says things that people would like to say but don't, and gets in trouble because of it. She's a fantastic opportunity for an actress.'

Turner began her career at the age of six, when she appeared in commercials. In her teens, she starred in a children's drama, *Into the Labyrinth*, for three years before reaching a crossroads in her life. 'I really wanted to do a course in musical theatre and swap over on to a drama course. But I couldn't get a grant, so I had

to pay for it myself out of the money I had earned as a child. I lasted a term; it cost me £2000 and I always thought it was a complete waste of money.'

'She says things that people would like to say but don't'

Turner's scepticism was born out of having had an excellent teacher before, the same drama teacher who taught actors Juliet Stevenson and Robert Lindsay. Yet, when she dropped out of her course, Turner did something neither of them ever did: 'I dyed my hair blonde and got a job as a dancer on Bruce Forsyth's show at the London Palladium. I danced there for about a year and then went on tour with bands like Rose Royce, Imagination and Level 42.' She groans: 'And it gets worse. I toured with the Grumbleweeds, the Drifters and the Nolan Sisters, too!'

Despite the dodgy music, Turner had a fantastic time, travelling as far afield as Cyprus and Norway. However, it wasn't long until her yearning to be an actress surfaced once more. She got a place at drama school and, on graduating, landed a job with a theatre company; she has been working ever since.

Television was effectively new territory for Turner when she decided to break into it: 'I decided the only way to do it was not to accept any theatre work and sit tight and wait for auditions for TV to come up.' Luckily, it wasn't too long before Turner was offered the part of Gina: 'I was so pleased,' Turner admits, 'I just hope it continues to be so much fun. I think it will be. Gina's full of surprises...'

'And the Winner is...' – Award Photos

On the night of the National TV Awards the Bad Girls cast gathered in a central London hotel to indulge in some pre-award ceremony drinks in an attempt to calm their nerves. But, try as they might, the cast couldn't quite leave behind the habits of the Larkhall characters they play every day.

These pictures were taken before they found out Bad Girls had won the coveted National TV Award for best drama. (Unfortunately we can't print the pictures taken after they won!)

1 'Miss, can I see what's in your swinger?' 2 Zandra demonstrates the Boston Arm Lock to Bodybag
3 'Get your hand off my bum, Mr Fenner' 4 'Keep smiling, I'm nicking his wallet'

5 "Scuse me, Miss, this is cons only' 6 'Don't look now, but I think she fancies you
7 Has Shell Dockley put something in their tea? 8 All together now: 'What a friend we have in Jesus'
9 The idea is to get both hands round his neck and squeeze 10 'When I give the signal, leg it through that skylight up there'

Supporting Cast
– Ancillary Characters

SEAN PARR
More Affectionately Known As:
Sean the Prawn
Distinguishing Features:
No backbone
Likes: Weeping willows
Dislikes: Fire-proof suits

RACHEL HICKS
More Affectionately Known As:
Oi, Hicks
Distinguishing Features:
'Victim' stamped on forehead
Likes: Very, very bright red lipstick
Dislikes: Shell's drawings

JESSIE DEVLIN
More Affectionately Known As:
Denny's Mum
Distinguishing Features:
Thrift-shop clothes
Likes: A fella with a six-pack
Dislikes: Licensing hours

TESSA SPALL
More Affectionately Known As:
Mad
Distinguishing Features:
Can look both ways at the same time
Likes: Tap-dancing, hymns
Dislikes: Colonic irrigation

RENEE WILLIAMS
More Affectionately Known As:
The Nutter
Distinguishing Features:
Iguana eyes
Likes: Chewing razor blades
Dislikes: Orange juice past its sell-by date; nuts

ROBIN DUNSTAN
More Affectionately Known As:
Bastard
Distinguishing Features:
Serial fiancé
Likes: Mummy's home cooking
Dislikes: Has gone off heroin lately

BOBBY HOLLAMBY
More Affectionately Known As:
Bobbybag
Distinguishing Features:
Overgrown sideburns
Likes: Braised meatballs
Dislikes: His wife on E

CHARLIE ATKINS
More Affectionately Known As:
Dead-End Charlie
Distinguishing Features: Bullet hole in the head
Likes: Slappers
Dislikes: Pizza takeaways

DR NICHOLSON
More Affectionately Known As:
Dr No-No
Distinguishing Features:
Locked medicine cupboard
Likes: An easy life
Dislikes: Prisoners

MARILYN FENNER
More Affectionately Known As:
Marilyn the Martyr
Distinguishing Features:
Furrowed brow
Likes: Crease-free clothes
Dislikes: Anonymous phone calls

PAMELA JOLLY
More Affectionately Known As:
Podger
Distinguishing Features:
Built like a slightly deflated bouncy castle
Likes: Cuddly kittens
Dislikes: Shell in the showers

THE CHAPLAIN
More Affectionately Known As:
Happy Clappy Chappie
Distinguishing Features: Halo
Likes: Psalm 23
Dislikes: The devil and all his works

THE POTTING SHED
More Affectionately Known As:
Its Latin name, *Grabbus Breastus Primus Locationus*
Distinguishing Features:
Seen more action than an Arnold Schwarzenegger movie
Likes: Love trysts
Dislikes: Snooping screws

Speaking the Language – Glossary

Adjudication Occurs after prisoners break rules. A governor-grade officer will decide upon the appropriate punishment in a formal hearing with the prisoner present.

A.P.S. Accelerated Promotion Scheme. This is a fast-track opportunity for graduates, like Helen Stewart, to achieve governor grade, usually within five years.

Association A period of time in which the inmates may integrate for recreation.

Basic Prisoners are graded under the Incentives and Earned Privileges Scheme. The entry level is Basic – which allows minimal freedom of movement, visits, income and facilities. In Larkhall, prisoners on the Basic regime are housed on the ground floor: the 'Ones', often in shared cells.

Block Segregation unit for inmates who break rules.

Canteen The prison shop, where prisoners can buy allowed items of food, toiletries, phone cards etc. with their personal spends and wages.

C.C.R.C. Criminal Cases Review Commission.

Closed Visits: A security measure requiring the prisoner to meet her visitors behind a screen and under supervision.

Compact A deal struck between prisoners and officers, which is usually beneficial to both.

Crutching Smuggling in contraband, often drugs, by hiding it internally.

Decrutching The act – often violent – of forcibly removing the item that someone has hidden internally.

The Dorm The four-bunk double cell on G1 landing. Should be avoided at all costs, as it has previously housed the ill-fated Rachel Hicks, Zandra Plackett and Renee Williams.

D.S.T. Dedicated Search Team. Special group of officers who are trained and equipped to search for drugs and other contraband. Also known as the 'swoop squad' or 'squat team'.

Enhanced Enhanced regime incorporates single cells with better furnishings, mostly on the top landing: the 'Threes'. Inmates also have greater freedom of movement, can receive more visits and get more personal spends. Or, as Nikki puts it, 'a few extra quid and a duvet'.

Girls Officers' term for all women prisoners, irrespective of age.

G.O.A.D. Written shorthand for 'Good Order and Discipline'.

Jellies Temazepam, an anti-depressant drug.

M.D.T. Mandatory Drugs Testing. Prisoners are selected at random, usually by computer, to provide a urine sample. Tests are also required on reception, or if there is 'reasonable suspicion'. Generally referred to as 'the piss test'.

Red Bands: Trusted prisoners given the better jobs within the prison – a privilege often abused.

Rule 43 One of the Prison Rules, under which an unruly inmate is removed to the segregation unit for the maintenance of Good Order and Discipline.

Servery Where the prisoners are served their meals. Also a great place for a fight or secret liaison.

Standard Most inmates are on this intermediate regime and are usually housed on the second landing: the 'Twos'.

Strips Punishment on the Block, where a prisoner's clothing is removed and replaced by a garment made of untearable paper – that 'blue dress thing' as modelled by Nikki.

Swinger A rope made of knotted sheets or clothing, often with plastic bag attached, swung from one cell window to another to convey illicit items.

V.O. Visiting Order. Prisoners must send a V.O. out to their intended visitors